FRIDA KAHLO AND DIEGO RIVERA

from the
Jacques and Natasha Gelman Collection

ART GALLERY NSW

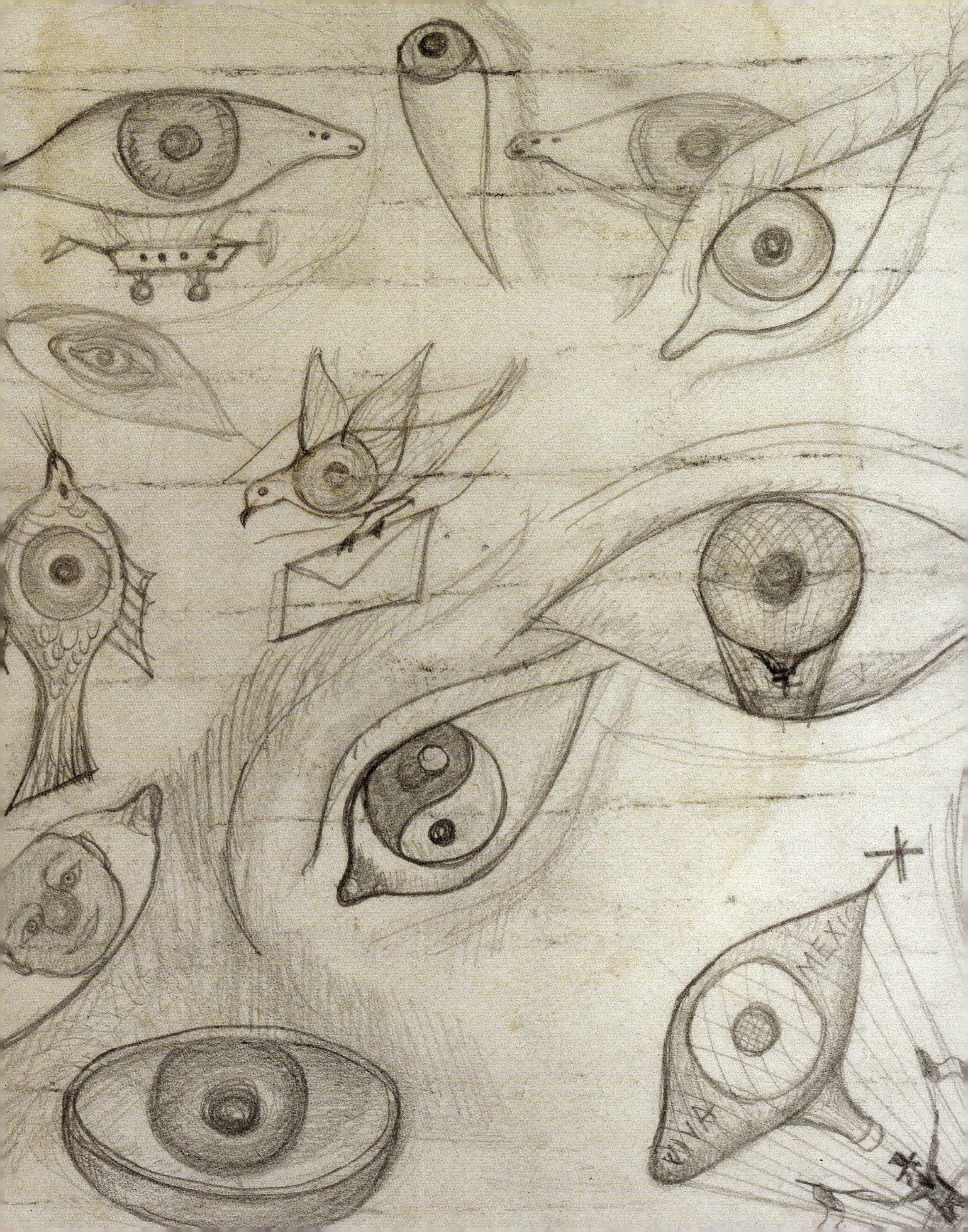
VIVA
MEXICO

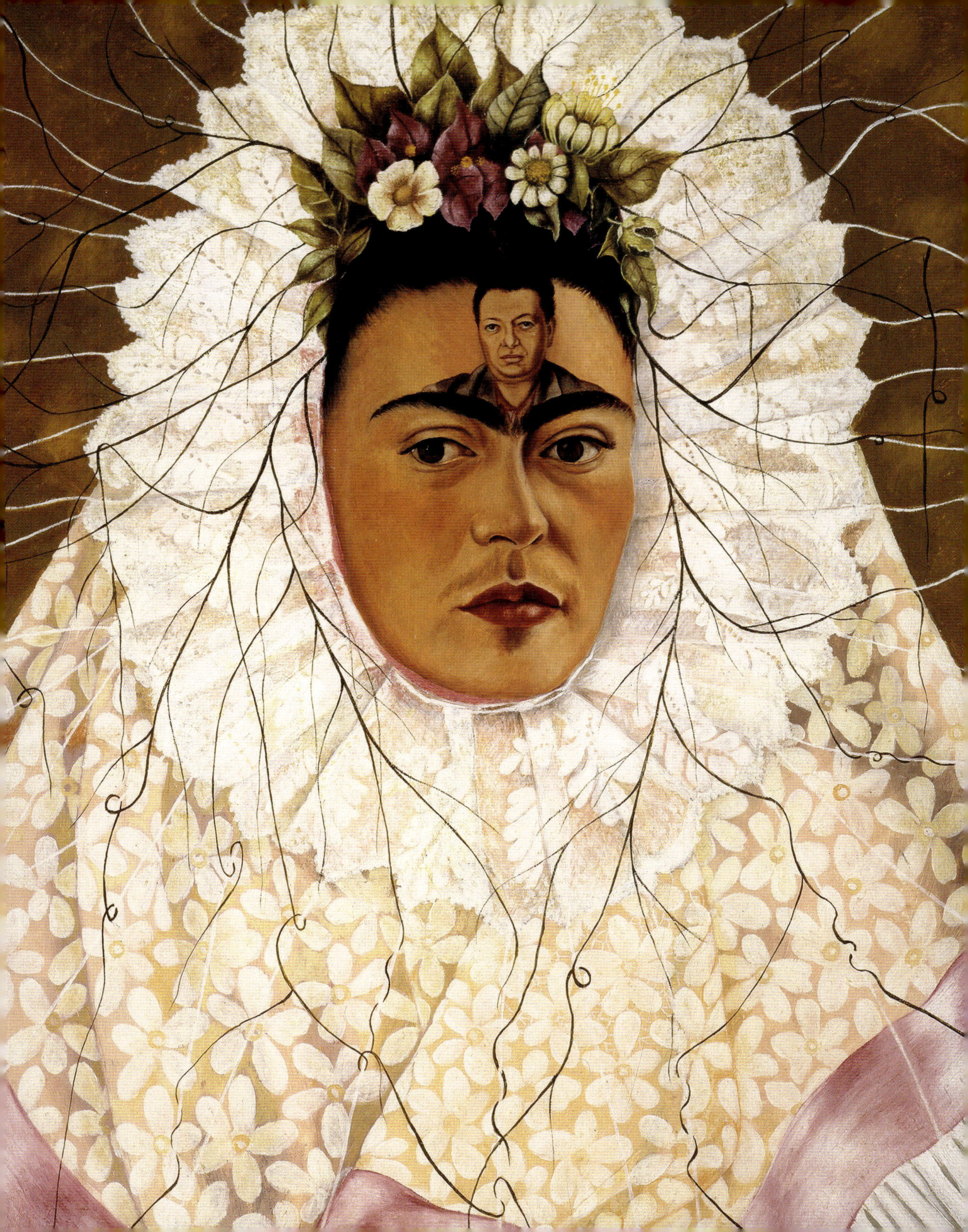

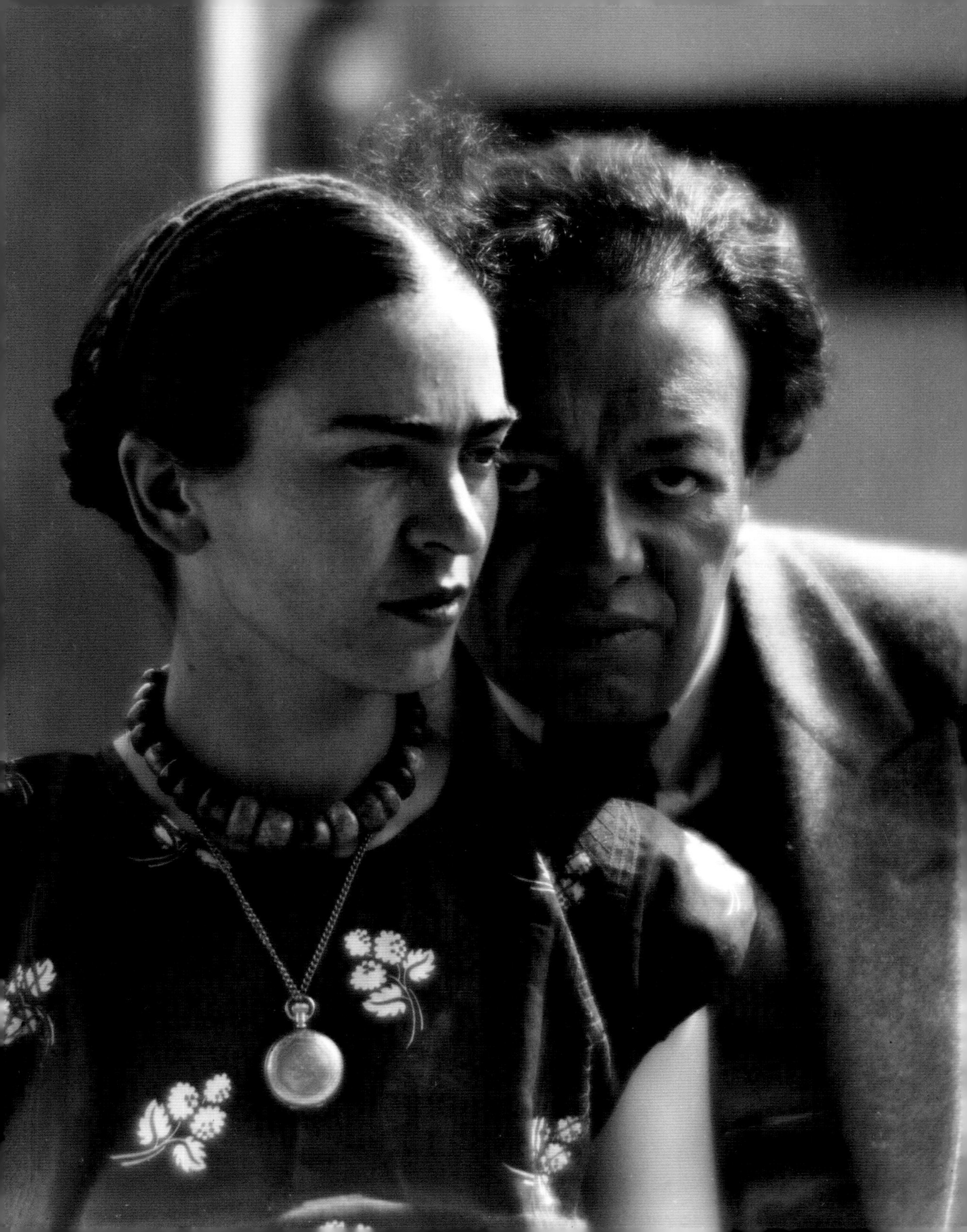

Foreword

The Art Gallery of New South Wales is delighted to present *Frida Kahlo and Diego Rivera: from the Jacques and Natasha Gelman Collection*. It has been more than a decade since either Kahlo or Rivera's work has been seen in depth in this country and, with no paintings by either artist in an Australian museum collection, the exhibition presents an important opportunity for audiences across the nation. Bringing together major works by both Kahlo and Rivera, the exhibition places the artists in a dialogue – one which this publication expands upon through the reprinting of Rivera's 1943 essay 'Frida Kahlo and Mexican Art' and Kahlo's 'Portrait of Diego', written on the occasion of her husband's 1949 retrospective. Together, the exhibition and publication reveal the artists' fiercely independent artistic visions while also pointing to political, cultural and personal concerns that affected them both.

Importantly, the exhibition includes Kahlo and Rivera's portraits of Natasha Gelman, both commissioned by her husband Jacques in 1943. European émigrés who met in Mexico City and became Mexican citizens, the Gelmans built a collection that is today regarded as the most important private holding of Mexican modern art.

The exhibition also features a group of photographs from the collection of Throckmorton Fine Art, New York, by figures such as Edward Weston, Lola Alvarez Bravo and Guillermo Kahlo, Frida's father. Spanning from 1928 until Kahlo's death in 1954, the photographs add another dimension to Kahlo and Rivera's art practices and help to relate the extraordinary story of their life together.

The Gallery is indebted to The Vergel Foundation, the custodians of the Gelman Collection, and particularly its president and director, Robert R Littman, for his generosity in lending such superb works of art, as well as its curator, Magda Carranza de Akle, for her great assistance in coordinating this exhibition. I would also like to acknowledge John Yeoh from Artémios who provided invaluable support in the development of this exhibition. I extend my sincere thanks to the Gallery's President's Council for generously supporting this exhibition and to their ongoing support which contributes greatly to the Gallery's ability to present ambitious and stimulating exhibitions in Sydney.

MICHAEL BRAND
Director, Art Gallery of New South Wales

Diego observing Frida paint 'Self-portrait on the borderline', Detroit 1932
Photographer unknown

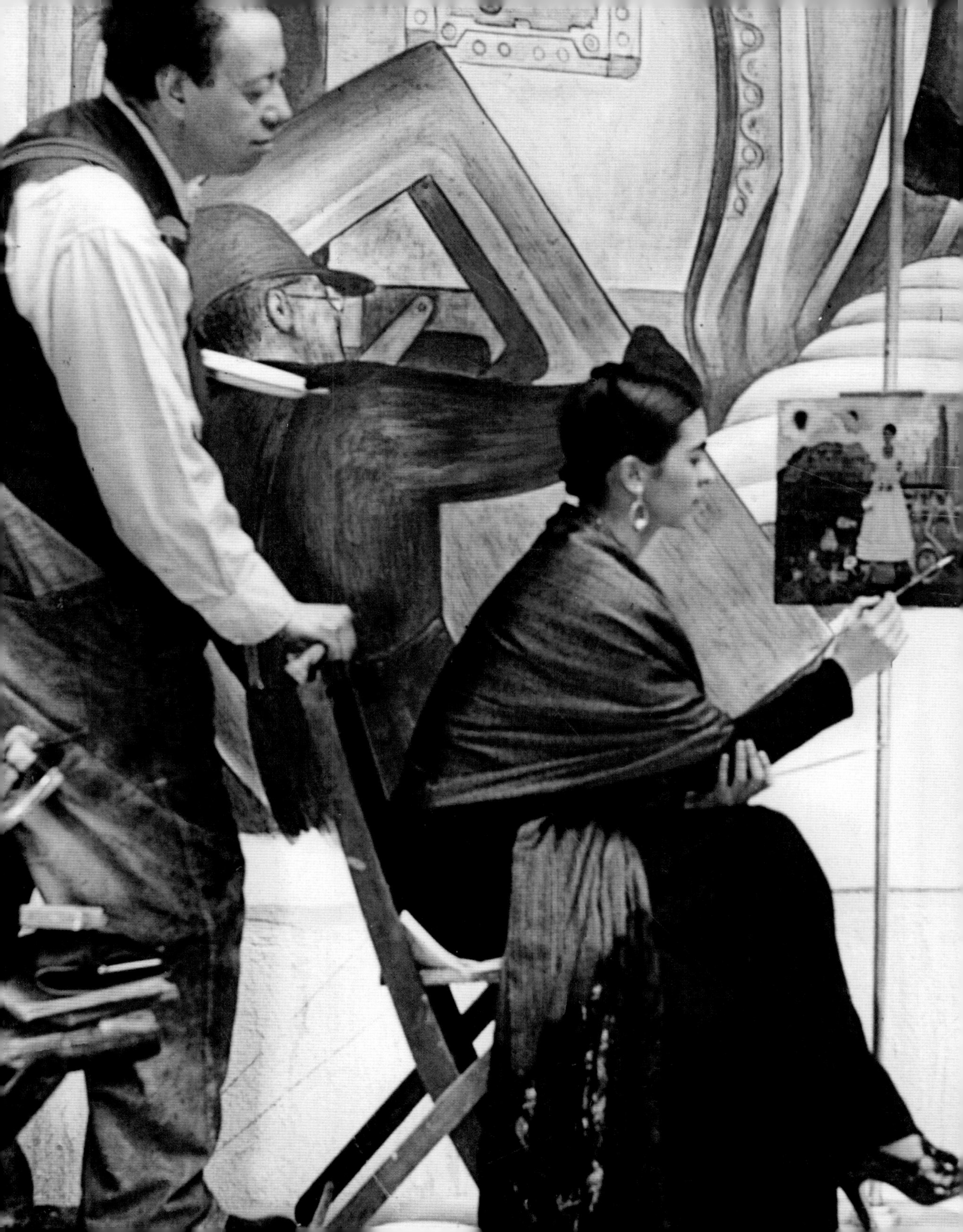

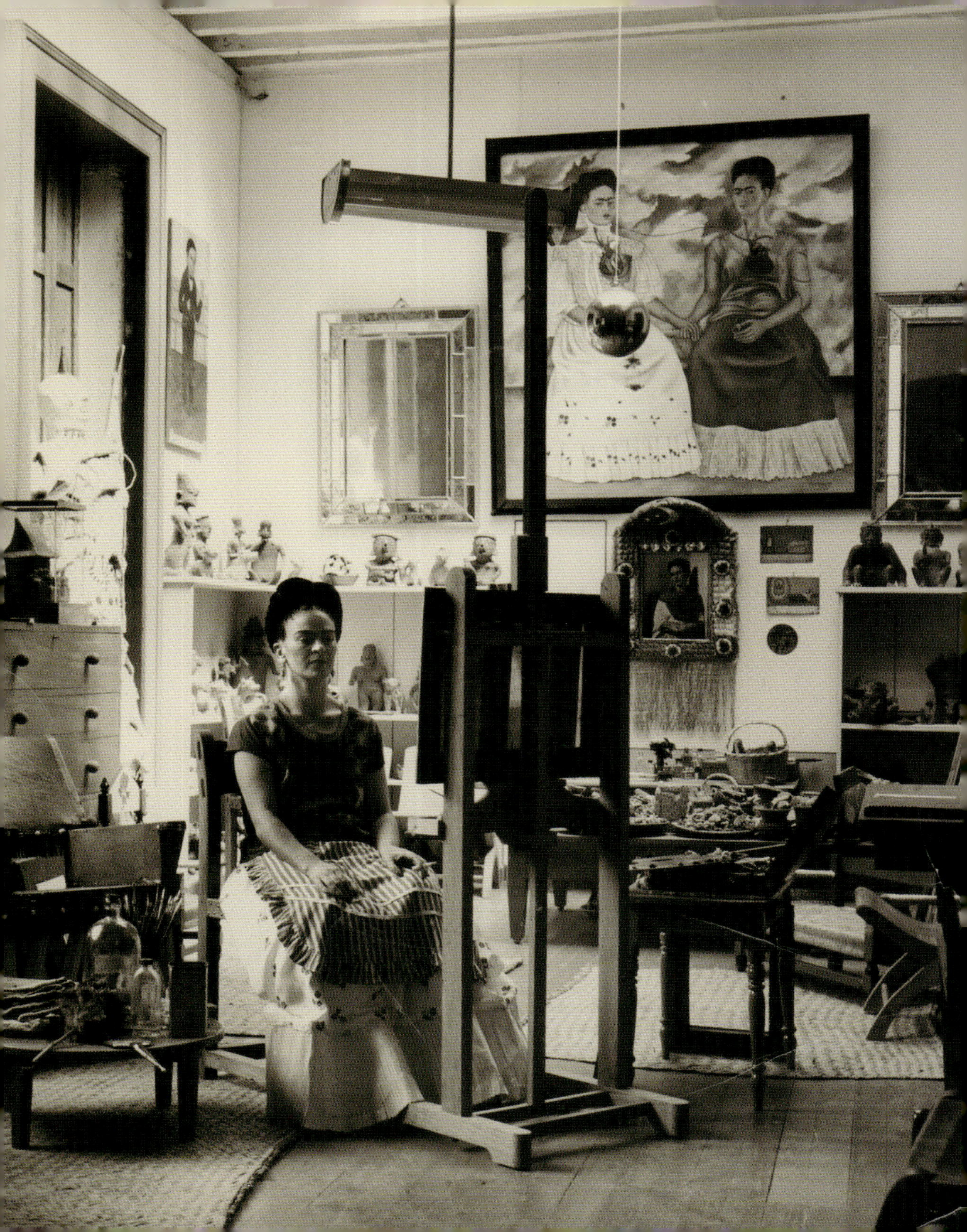

Jacques and Natasha Gelman

During the twenty years of my life in Mexico, my friendship with both Jacques and Natasha Gelman was a determining factor to my cultural transition from life in New York City. After Jacques' death in 1986, Natasha and I increasingly shared time together, as I lived only one hour away in Mexico City and she in Cuernavaca. During my last visit with her, the weekend before she died, we went for lunch to her favourite restaurant, a converted seventeenth-century manor house whose facade hides a tropical paradise with luscious gardens and wandering troops of white peacocks and yellow tufted herons. Natasha asked for her usual table adjacent to the entrance where she could analyse and succinctly comment on the manner and character of those clients entering and leaving. That perceptiveness and direct observation pretty much sums up the actual way the Gelmans collected: without hesitation and without regard to the opinion of others and always on target.

Natasha and Jacques Gelman acquired the canvases of Frida Kahlo and her husband, Diego Rivera, when there were only a handful of collectors in Mexico. When the Gelmans became enthusiastic about an artist's work, they reinforced their convictions (as well as the artist's financial well-being) by buying in depth the work of those so favoured. It just so happened these artists came to be the most famous of their generation. Natasha's great beauty was documented by the portraits her adoring husband commissioned by these same artists. One could fill a whole gallery just with these portraits.

Natasha had a very clear idea and mission of what was needed to complete and strengthen the collection housed in Mexico and New York on Jacques' death. Not only did she use her connaissance to complete what works she felt were needed in the collection of School of Paris painting and sculpture, which went to the Metropolitan Museum of Art on her death, but she concentrated an equal amount of energy in keeping her Mexican collection up to date. One can take, for example, the late addition to the collection of an important oil by Frida Kahlo, *The love embrace of the universe*. The collection was placed throughout the rooms of her house in Cuernavaca and lived with and enjoyed continually.

Natasha died peacefully the morning of 4 May 1998 in her house in Cuernavaca, where, as on every morning, she would have seen the peak of Popocatépetl from her bedroom window and faced her selection of self-portraits by Kahlo. She was eighty-six years old.

This collection is still a work-in-progress, as it was for Natasha and Jacques Gelman during their lifetimes. In the years following her death, twelve new works by Frida Kahlo were added – all the works on paper shown in the exhibition. A brief exhibition in Paris of this collection ensued after Natasha's death and had been organised in tribute to the Gelmans. Thanks to its initial critical acclaim and popularity, the exhibition extended into a continuing four-continent tour and now these paintings, drawings and photographs come to Sydney.

Fritz Henle
Frida in her studio
1943

ROBERT R LITTMAN
President and director of The Vergel Foundation

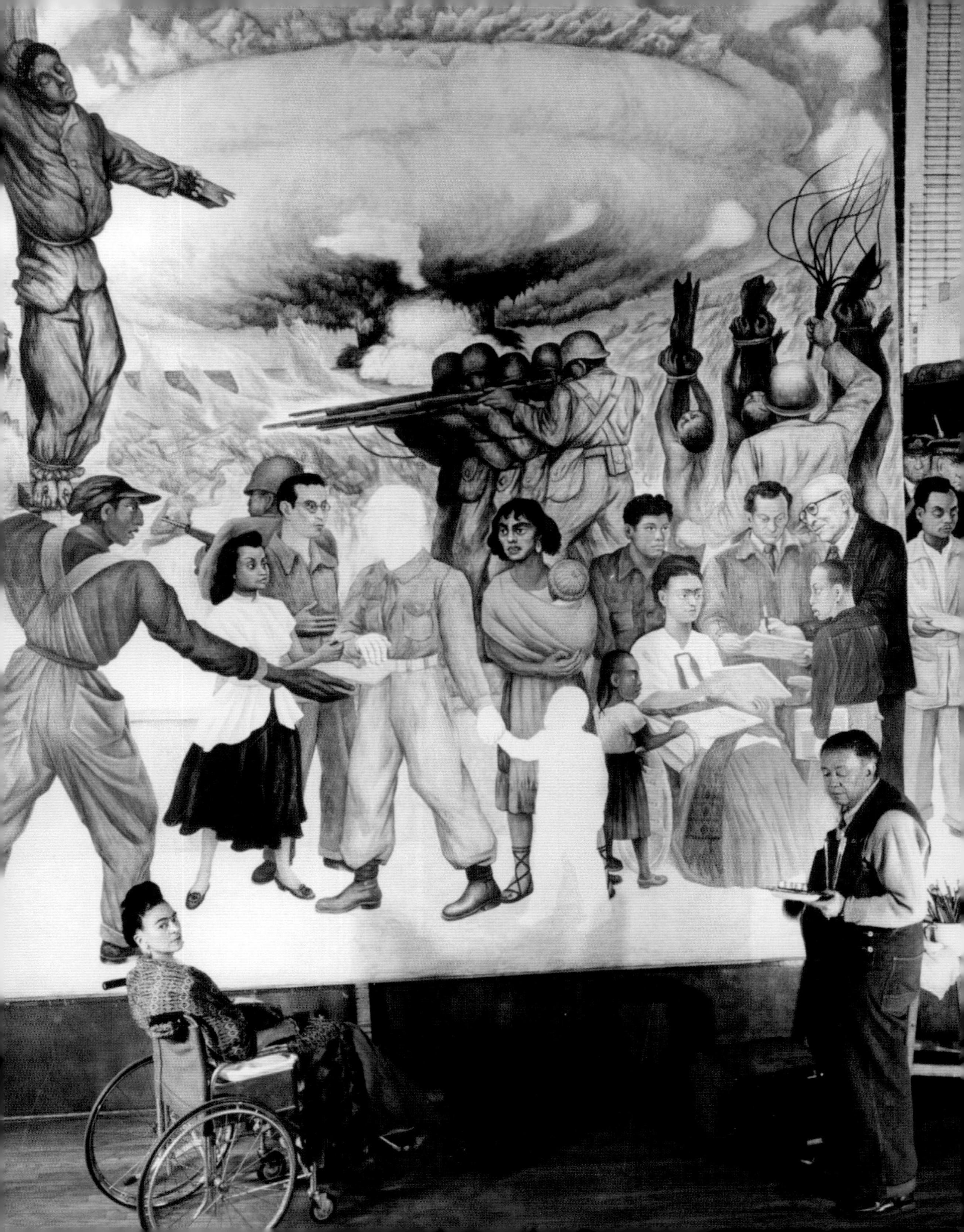

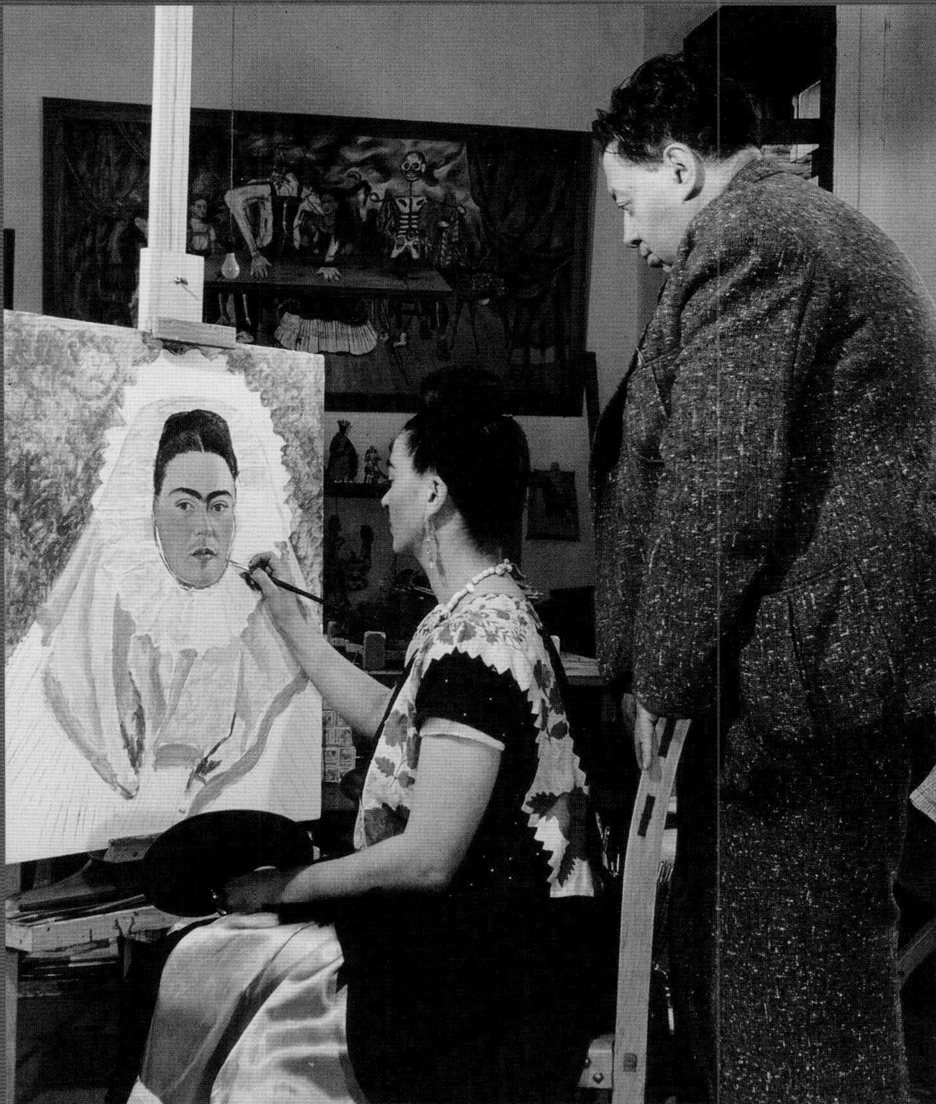

–

Bernard Silberstein
Frida paints self-portrait while Diego observes 1940

–

opposite: Juan Guzmán
Frida and Diego by mural 'The nightmare of war and the dream of peace', the Palace of Fine Arts, Mexico 1952

Frida Kahlo and Diego Rivera

–

NICHOLAS CHAMBERS

–

During their lifetimes, Frida Kahlo and Diego Rivera achieved a combination of public admiration and critical acclaim that has been afforded only to a small group of twentieth-century artists. Even fewer have continued to captivate and provoke audiences more than half a century after their deaths. When they married in 1929, Rivera's influence in Mexico and regard overseas was rapidly ascending while Kahlo, twenty years her husband's junior, had not yet publicly exhibited her artwork. It is not the case, however, that Kahlo's practice developed in the shadow of Rivera's. As Rivera himself recognised, and attested to in the 1943 essay reprinted in this publication, Kahlo was regarded during her lifetime as a major figure in Mexican painting – albeit one who had a dramatically different sensibility to Rivera and the social realism that he, his peers and, indeed, the state of Mexico championed.

While Rivera's art projected itself outwards, often on a vast scale, and concerned itself with the construction of a national identity in post-revolutionary Mexico, Kahlo's turned inwards and represented Mexicanidad through an exploration of her personal identity. The marked differences between the two artists' output meant that, until recently, there had been few major museum exhibitions juxtaposing their practices. This exhibition, made possible by the Jacques and Natasha Gelman Collection, speaks to the artistic dialogue between Kahlo and Rivera while emphasising their fierce independence and the uniqueness of their artistic visions. It highlights the manner in which their stylistically and conceptually divergent approaches to painting are able to reflect on common themes: from the dramatic story of their life together to their shared investment in the cultural life of Mexico.

Diego Rivera was born in the central Mexican city of Guanajuato, but his family moved to Mexico City when he was still very young. A precocious talent, he attended the Academy of San Carlos and received a sound education in drawing and painting. Rivera's first artworks were deeply influenced by his teacher, José María Velasco, whose landscape paintings had made Mexican geography a symbol of the nation's identity in the nineteenth century. In 1907, at the age of twenty, Rivera left for Europe, initially living in Madrid before settling in Paris where he became involved in the ferment of the European avant-garde and began painting in a Cubist style. At the outbreak of war in 1914, Rivera was visiting the Spanish island of Mallorca where he executed several major cubist compositions including *Last hour* 1915 (p 65), which was among the first paintings by Rivera to be acquired by the Gelmans. The earthy tones of this painting, its textured surface and integration of text bear

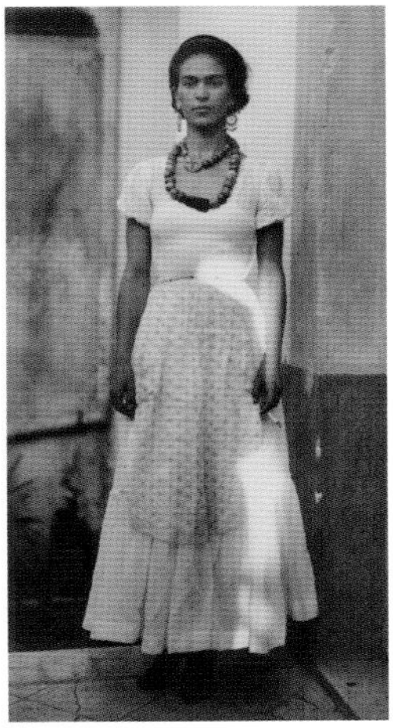

left:

Guillermo Davila
Frida 1929

right:

Guillermo Zamora
Frida and Diego, Coyoacán
1937

Manuel Alvarez Bravo
Frida at the Society of Modern Art, Picasso exhibit, Mexico
c1944

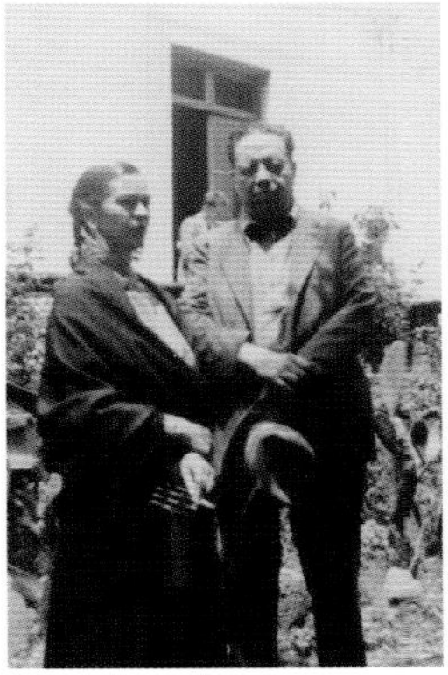

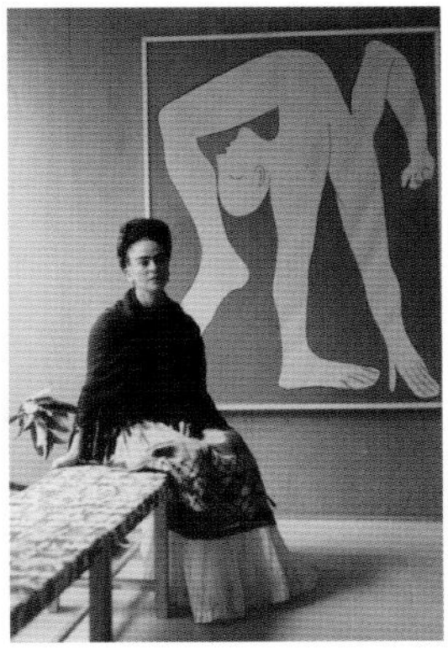

comparison to contemporary works by Georges Braque and Pablo Picasso. According to Rivera's lover at the time, artist Marevna, 'Picasso used to come by to Rivera's studio and wander about freely, turning over the canvases at will to look at them. Rivera complained to me more than once, "I'm sick of Picasso: if he pinches something from me, people will rave about Picasso, Picasso. As for me, they'll say I copy him. One of these days I'll chuck him out or I'll shove off to Mexico."'[1]

A trip to Italy in 1920–21, made possible by the Mexican Minister for Culture, José Vasconcelos, exposed Rivera to the Italian Renaissance frescoes of the quattrocento and proved to be a crucial step in the development of his career. Vasconcelos had recently initiated the Mexican mural painting movement with the commissioning of Roberto Montenegro and Xavier Guerrero to paint murals in the former monastery of San Pedro and San Pablo. In 1921, at the minister's request, Rivera returned to Mexico to contribute to the mural program; as fate would have it, his first project was an auditorium at the National Preparatory School where Kahlo had just been admitted as a student.

Kahlo was born in Coyoacán, a suburb on the southern outskirts of Mexico City, to German photographer Guillermo Kahlo, a Mexican resident, and Matilde Calderón, from Oaxaca. Kahlo's childhood was spent in Coyoacán and the downtown neighbourhoods of the capital, where her father had a photography studio. A rebellious child with a prodigious intellect, Kahlo was one of only thirty-five girls out of 2000 students admitted to the prestigious National Preparatory School where she witnessed Rivera painting the aforementioned mural. In 1925 her life was irrevocably altered when she was travelling in a bus that was violently struck by a tram, causing Kahlo to break her spinal column, ribs, pelvis and collarbone. She was temporarily immobilised in a body cast but during this period made her first paintings on a specially fabricated easel that enabled her to paint while confined to a bed. Over two years Kahlo made a remarkable recovery but was left with spinal injuries for which she would have to undergo numerous operations for the rest of her life.

As her health improved, Kahlo became increasingly involved in artistic and political circles in Mexico City and forged an important friendship with the Italian-American photographer Tina Modotti, Edward Weston's assistant at the time. Through Modotti she joined the Mexican Communist Party, which had been outlawed by the government of Plutarco Elías Calles in 1925 but nevertheless continued underground and counted many leading muralists, including Rivera, as members. Modotti likely introduced Kahlo to Rivera in 1928. Their courtship reportedly proceeded apace, with Rivera visiting Kahlo at her family's house on Sunday afternoons and Kahlo spending more and more time accompanying Rivera on the scaffold as he worked on his mural cycle for the Ministry of Education.

On 21 August 1929, just months after the establishment of the National Revolutionary Party which brought political stability to post-revolutionary Mexico, Kahlo and Rivera were married in Coyoacán. Kahlo's parents are said to have objected both to Rivera's politics and portly figure, and expressed their disapproval of the marriage by describing it as the union of a dove and an elephant.[2] Shortly after the wedding, Rivera was expelled from the Mexican Communist Party, ostensibly for accepting a mural commission from the Calles government. Kahlo immediately left the party in protest.

In 1930, in what must have seemed as vindication for the Mexican Communist Party, the two artists moved to the United States where Rivera began work on a mural for the San Francisco Stock Exchange Luncheon Club. They would subsequently spend three years in the United States, during which time Rivera was preoccupied with numerous commissions and a major solo exhibition at the Museum of Modern Art (MoMA), New York. Held in 1931, it was MoMA's second single-artist retrospective, after Henri Matisse, and set a new attendance record. Rivera created a series of new paintings on canvas, including the anthropomorphic *Landscape with cacti* 1931 (pp 68–69), in which two cacti appear to vie for the attention of a third with breast-like branches. Some commentators have speculated that the painting alludes to the relationship between Rivera, Kahlo and photographer Nickolas Muray, with whom Kahlo had recently started an affair. The composition is also arguably indebted to the sensuous desert landscapes depicted in the photographs of Edward Weston, who was known to Rivera and lived in Mexico from 1923–26.

Rivera's demanding schedule left Kahlo, whose own artistic career was not yet established, in a rather isolated position. In *The sun peeks through the window* 1932 (p 47), Kahlo depicts the view from her hotel room in New York, which she visited for the opening of Rivera's 1931 exhibition. As Helga Prignitz-Poda, author of the Frida Kahlo catalogue raisonné, has noted, the dreary colours she inscribed onto the various parts of the composition – 'grey, brown, shades of brick' – are punctuated by a radiating sun which is both witness to and symbol of her feeling of homesickness.

Much of 1932 was spent in Detroit where Rivera was painting *Detroit industry* 1932–33, a sequence of murals at the Detroit Institute of Arts. Kahlo was expecting the birth of her first child but suffered a miscarriage at the Henry Ford Hospital. She subsequently created two works of art as a way of both analysing and coping with this traumatic event: a painting, *Henry Ford Hospital* 1932, and a lithograph, *The miscarriage* 1932 (p 46), two imprints of which are included in the exhibition. Kahlo's friend, artist Lucienne Bloch, who was assisting Rivera with the murals, related the story of the lithograph:

> *Back at her apartment at The Wardell Hotel, Frida was suffering from such a heavy depression that Diego asked me to stay with her. We decided to do something together and wanted to take advantage of the applied arts studio near the hotel. I wrote in my journal on 24 July 1932: 'how well everything seems to progress, we arrived at nine o'clock. The caretaker showed us the lithograph workshop with the large press and stones … Frida drew the scenes of her bleeding, the fetus, and the cell divisions directly onto her stone. As soon as someone entered the studio to see what we were "playing" with, she would behave like a wild animal. No one understood how seriously we were working.'*[3]

The resulting print shows Kahlo mourning her unborn child, her body divided vertically into light and dark halves, as if to suggest a split psyche. The left side of the composition is dominated by dividing cells and a male foetus connected to Kahlo by its umbilical cord. On the right side, blood from the haemorrhage that ended the pregnancy drips down her leg and appears to nourish plants,

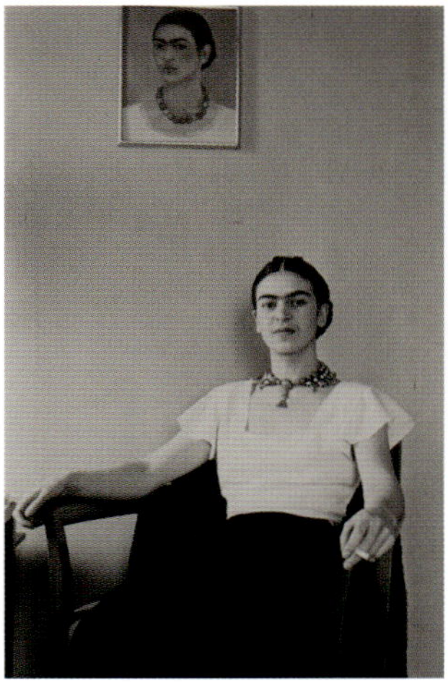

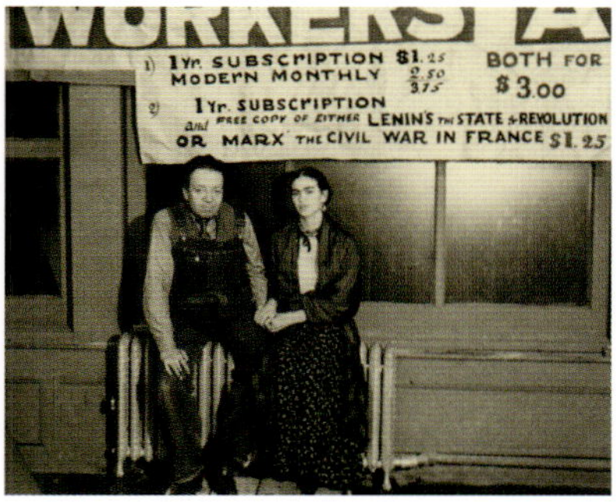

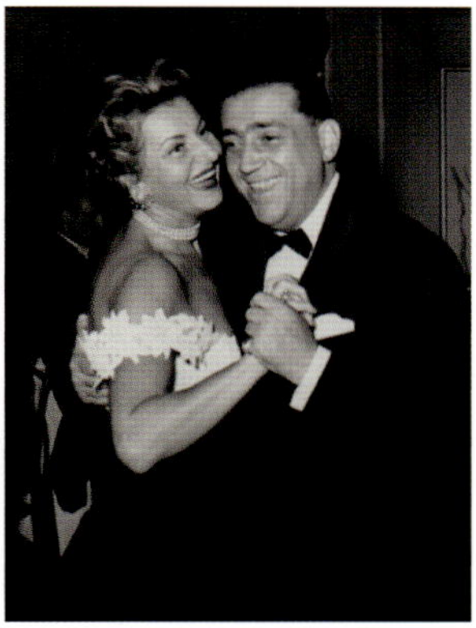

from left:

Frida at the Barbizon Plaza Hotel 1933; *New Workers School, NYC* 1933, Lucienne Bloch

Natasha and Jacques Gelman, photographer unknown, courtesy of the Gelman Collection

which resemble the eyes, hands and genitals of the foetus,[4] perhaps reconciling the miscarriage as part of a cycle of life, death and rebirth.

A year later, Kahlo and Rivera returned to Detroit where she painted *Self-portrait with necklace* 1933 (p 33). The earliest artwork by Kahlo in the exhibition, it was meticulously executed on metal, in the manner of a Mexican votive painting, and depicts the artist wearing a piece of pre-Columbian jade jewellery. Of particular note is the careful attention she paid to her face, using very fine brushwork to create a smooth, youthful complexion and to painstakingly represent her moustache and unibrow, symbols of her Mexican heritage. In Bloch's photograph *Frida at the Barbizon Plaza Hotel* 1933 (above), the artist is seated beneath this portrait aping the serious, dignified and highly self-aware expression portrayed in the painting.

In 1933 Kahlo and Rivera moved into a Mexico City studio and residence complex designed by Juan O'Gorman, which is the present-day home of the Studio Museum of Diego Rivera and Frida Kahlo. The subsequent years were highly productive for both – Rivera completed his renowned mural cycle, *Epic of the Mexican people* 1945–52, at the National Palace in Mexico City, and Kahlo's work became increasingly well-known both in Mexico and abroad. André Breton became a great admirer, including her work in an exhibition at Galerie Renou et Colle, Paris, from which the Louvre acquired her painting, *The frame* 1938 – the museum's first acquisition of a twentieth-century Mexican work, now held in the collection of the Centre Pompidou, Paris.

In 1941 Kahlo was appointed as a teacher at the National School of Painting, Sculpture and Printmaking (known as La Esmeralda) where Rivera was already a professor. *Self-portrait with red and gold dress* 1941 (p 35) commemorates this event in a rather ironic fashion. The mottled brown ground of the painting, into which Kahlo's name and the date 'MCMXLI' is grandiosely inscribed, evokes the plaster substrate of a mural painting; her pose is that of a serious academic yet her doctoral cap is fashioned from braided hair like that worn by the rural Tehuana women of South Mexico. The overall impression is one of gently mocking the academy to which she has now become a part.

It was around this time that Jacques and Natasha Gelman encountered Kahlo and Rivera. The Gelmans had met in Mexico City in 1939 but were both born in Europe, Natasha in Bohemia (present-day Czech Republic) and Jacques in Russia. Raised in St Petersburg in a well-to-do bourgeois family, Jacques left Russia following the 1917 Bolshevik Revolution. He first lived in Berlin where he studied cinema and later moved to Paris where he established his own film distribution company. In 1938, on the eve of World War II, Jacques travelled to Mexico

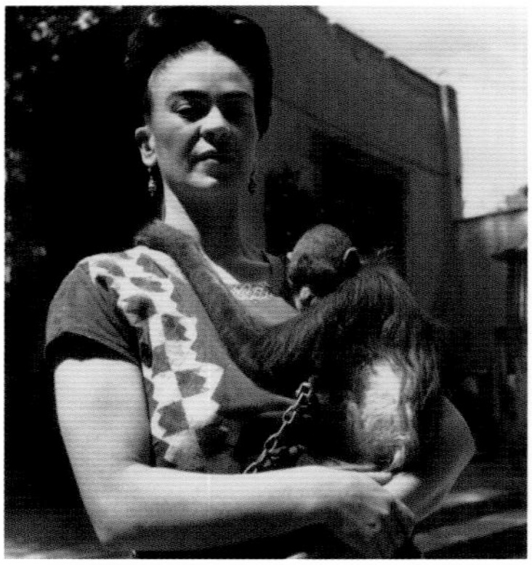

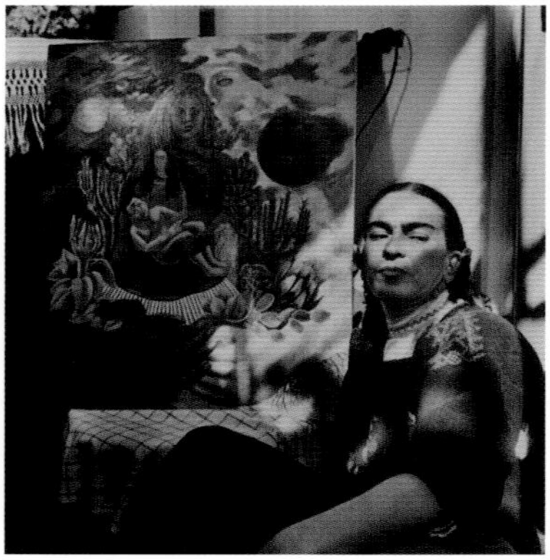

Fritz Henle
Frida in front of studio with monkey, Coyoacán 1943

Héctor García
Frida with painting ('The love embrace') 1949

with the view to establishing a new branch of his company that could cater to the Spanish-speaking nations of Central and South America. With the outbreak of war in Europe, Jacques decided to stay in Mexico City and ultimately became a partner in Posa Films – one of the leading Mexican film houses of the mid twentieth century. Jacques and Natasha married in 1941 and shortly thereafter became Mexican citizens.

The first Mexican painting to be purchased by the Gelmans was Rivera's *Portrait of Natasha Gelman* 1943 (pp 76–77), commissioned by Jacques. Natasha is portrayed in a luxurious white dress with a daring knee-high split that echoes the form of the calla lilies arranged behind her. The Gelmans also acquired *Calla lilly vendor* 1943 (p 75), depicting one of Rivera's most recognisable themes, as a partner to the portrait. This was not, however, the first time that Rivera had painted Natasha. She had previously been among a group of women who posed for Rivera's mural at the fashionable Mexico City nightclub, Ciro's. According to Rivera's grandson, Juan Rafael Coronel Rivera, the 'pin-up girl' style in which the models were represented raised Kahlo's ire. Coronel went on to speculate that Kahlo's displeasure with this incident may have influenced what he describes as Kahlo's 'malicious' 1943 painting *Portrait of Natasha Gelman* (p 43).[5] In this painting, also commissioned by Jacques and the first work he acquired from Kahlo, Natasha is represented as a highly fashionable yet dour woman. Her glamorous appearance, with elegantly plucked eyebrows and freshly curled waves of hair, evokes the modern look of 1940s movie stars and contrasts starkly with Kahlo's own self-image. Kahlo was, perhaps, particularly mischievous in her depiction of two prominent forehead curls that could easily be read as a pair of devil's horns. If there were any negative sentiments between the artist and sitter they were soon put aside as Natasha subsequently developed a close relationship with Kahlo and acquired nine additional paintings including some of her most important self-portraits.

In 1943 Kahlo became a full professor at La Esmeralda. For Kahlo, who had not received any formal art education, this was an exceptionally high honour. In *Self-portrait with monkeys* 1943 (p 39) one finds yet another humorous reference to Kahlo's official recognition by the Mexican cultural establishment. The viewer is caught in a stare that is at once proud and all too aware of the irony of the appointment. Her white blouse, a traditional outfit worn by Yalalag women of her mother's native Oaxaca province, is fastened with the tassel of a doctoral cap – underlying Kahlo's pride not only in her achievements but also in her rural Mexican ancestry. This painting is also arguably the earliest manifestation of 'Fridamania', with the four adoring monkeys representing a group of students who so admired their teacher that they became known as Los Fridos.

Another major work by Kahlo from 1943, *Diego on my mind (Self-portrait as Tehuana)* (p 41), reveals the central importance of the artists' relationship even as Kahlo achieved considerable success and recognition independently. Kahlo depicted herself wearing a lace huipil, traditionally worn by Tehuana women on Sundays, the threads of which radiate outwards and intertwine with roots emanating from a floral wreath. The overall effect can be read in numerous ways: as an aura, a cracked mirror or, perhaps, an exposed nervous system. Her visage, however, is calm and focused, as if conjuring Rivera who appears on Kahlo's forehead with a similarly meditative expression.

The exhibition also includes four paintings by Rivera from the same year. Despite his increasing preoccupation with mural painting, Rivera maintained a studio where he planned large-scale commissions and produced works on canvas to supplement his income. Some canvases functioned as studies for details of murals while others, such as *The healer* 1943 (p 72), portrayed Mexican genre scenes that were highly sought after by collectors. *Sunflowers* 1943 (pp 70–71), however, depicts what is, for Rivera, an unusually surrealistic image in which a boy and girl, dwarfed by a pot of sunflowers, play with masks and dolls. Seen in the context of the Gelman collection, the girl, who holds a broken doll in her arms and looks forlornly at its dismembered leg, is strongly evocative of Kahlo's disquieting *Self-portrait with bed (Me and my doll)* 1937 (p 31), in which a naked doll, variously interpreted as representing the artist's alter ego or her difficulties with childbirth, is seated next to Kahlo on a crude straw bed.

Following the deaths of Kahlo (1954) and Rivera (1957), just one painting was added to the collection by Natasha Gelman. Kahlo's *The love embrace of the universe, the Earth (Mexico), Diego, me and Señor Xólotl* 1949 (p 51) assimilates Aztec, Hindu and Christian iconography, and reveals a pointed assessment of the artists' relationship by the end of the 1940s. The overall composition borrows from the art-historical motif of the Virgin and Child with St Anne in which the saint is depicted, often at an exaggerated scale, embracing both Mary and Jesus. In Kahlo's reworking of this well-known image, an elemental being emerges from the sky and earth to embrace four figures: the Aztec fertility goddess Cihuacoatl, Kahlo, Rivera and their beloved dog, Xólotl. Kahlo, a Tehuana Virgin Mary, nurses a fat, naked baby Rivera who bears the third eye and flame of Hindu deity, Shiva. Kahlo's interest in non-Western religions, particularly Buddhism and Hinduism, developed strongly during the 1940s, and in this and other works from the decade, she projects a world view in which different cultures and belief systems merge. The painting also represents a shift in the artists' relationship insofar that Rivera, whose physical person and artistic reputation towered over Kahlo at the beginning of their relationship, is now depicted as a defenceless child.

A revealing analogue of this inversion can also be found in Rivera's mural *Dream of a Sunday afternoon in the Alameda Central* 1947–48, which portrays a diverse cast of characters from Mexico's history taking a stroll through Alameda Park. In it Rivera depicts himself as a young boy with an adult Kahlo standing behind him, her left hand holding a Buddhist Yin-Yang symbol and her right resting maternally on Rivera's shoulder. As Kahlo wrote of Rivera in her diary, 'At every moment he is my child, my child born every moment, diary, from myself.'[6]

1. Marevna, quoted in *Frida Kahlo and Diego Rivera from the Gelman Collection*, Pera Müzesi, Istanbul, 2011, p 171.

2. Hayden Herrera, *Frida: A biography of Frida Kahlo*, Harper and Row, New York, 1972, p 99.

3. Lucienne Bloch, cited in H Prignitz-Poda, S Grimbert and A Kettenmann, *Frida Kahlo: Das Gesamtwerk*, Neue Kritik, Frankfurt, 1987, p 224.

4. Herrera, p 146.

5. Juan Rafael Coronel Rivera, quoted in *Frida Kahlo and Diego Rivera from the Gelman Collection*, Pera Müzesi, Istanbul, 2011, p 122.

6. Frida Kahlo, quoted in Dore Ashton, 'Mexican art of the twentieth century', in *Mexico: Splendors of thirty centuries*, Metropolitan Museum of Art, New York, 1990, p 693.

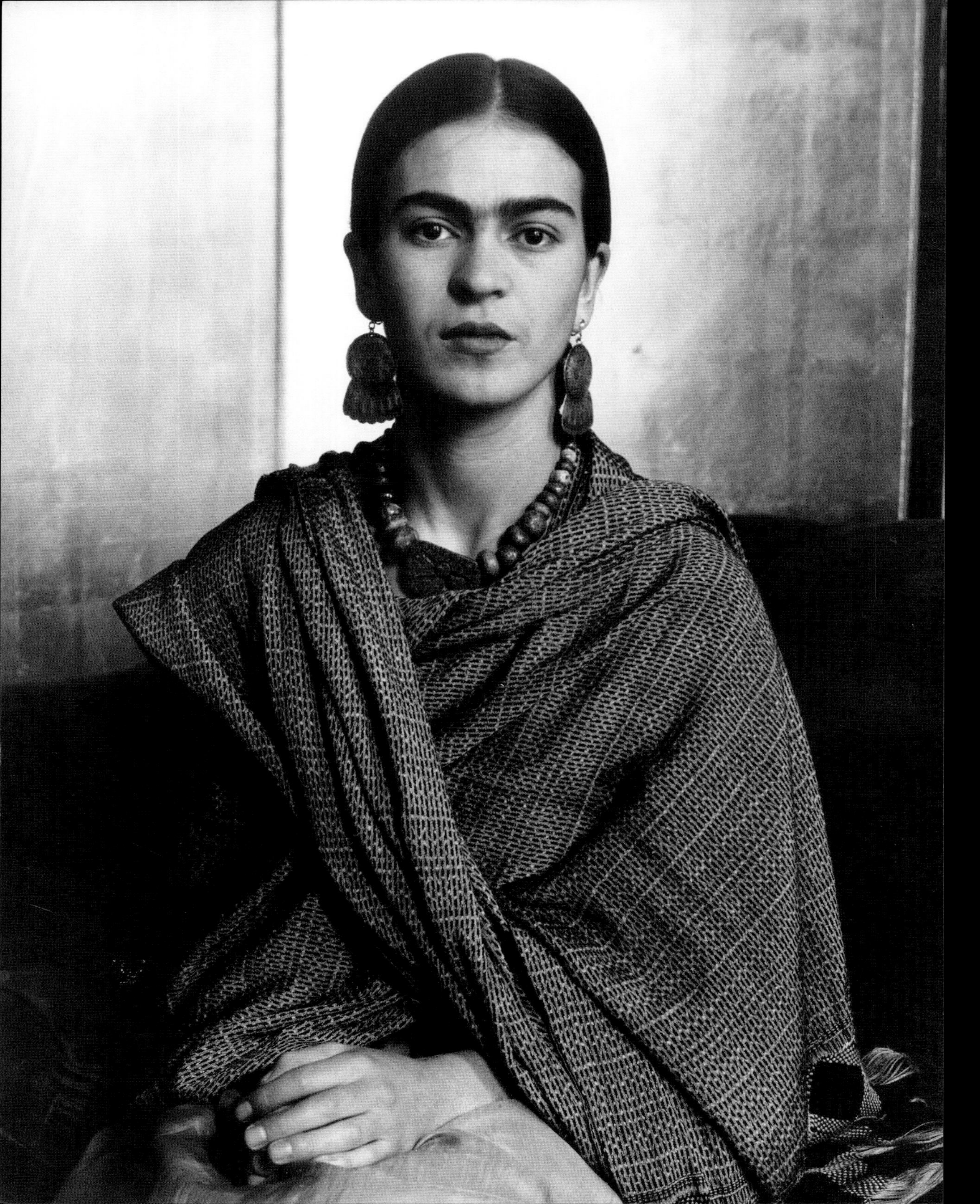

Frida

–

Imogen Cunningham
Frida Kahlo 1931

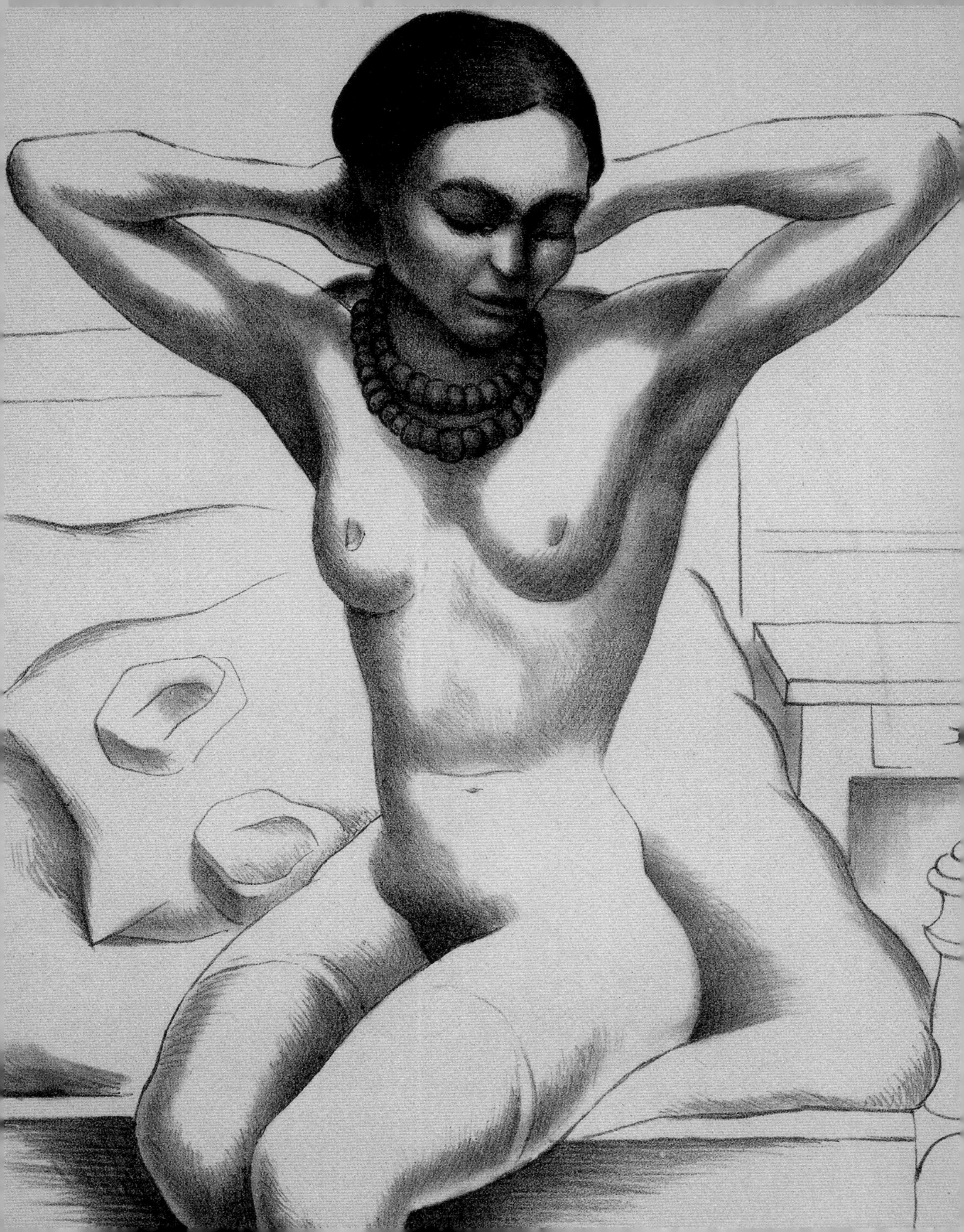

Frida Kahlo and Mexican art

–

BY DIEGO RIVERA

–

'Amid the panorama of all Mexican painting of quality produced in the last twenty years, the paintings of Frida Kahlo Calderón shine like clear, hard, precious ... diamonds in the centre of a great piece of jewellery.'

–

Mexico has been the meeting point of two strong and influential traditions of art: Native American Indian and Spanish. Apart from their relative position as the conqueror and the conquered, with its short-term economic consequences and medium-term idealogical and aesthetic repercussions, the nature of the elements of these two traditions have been and continue to be contradictory and impossible to amalgamate. When they are contained in the same work of a racially mixed art, they separate and lend the work a contradictory character in itself. On the other hand, this character determines a certain aspect of the originality of the work.

Sensual and mystical idealism is subjectified and translated into objective realism by Spanish art. From Juan Ruiz to Cervantes, from Saint Teresa of Ávila to Valle lnclán, from the Castilian, Aragon and Catalonian altarpieces, to Velázquez and Goya, and from Francisco de Zurbarán to El Greco and Picasso, the determining character has always been individual results.

On the part of Mexican art, this has been an occultist and poetic materialism – translated into a magical geometry – that uses signs rather than symbols to concretise itself into a monumental abstractive realism that extends beyond superficial, anatomical and descriptive objectivism, and attains the pure expression of superior proportions, the inherent movement of action and continuous formation during the quietism of *Life* itself ...

The elements of these traditions have always rebelled against amalgamation. Whenever an attempt is made to combine them, sooner or later, they break away from the emulsifying agent and separate like oil and water.

The emulsifying agent during the Spanish domination consisted of the imposing force of the conqueror and all that it possessed: the armed civil police, oral and written propaganda of the friars and doctors, the Laws of the Indies, By-laws of the Unions of New Spain, and particularly the powerful economic Law of *demand*. Naturally, this demand was determined by rich consumers, in other words, the administrators of the colony: *encomenderos*, religious and secular landowners, mine owners and concessionaries, patrons of industry and crafts, viceroys, judges, merchants, soldiers, clergymen and friars.[1] They all requested the products they preferred and rejected the ones that did not comply with their preferences or help protect or augment their interests. Unauthorised or disobedient producers were subjected to sanctions per the By-Laws of the Unions of New Spain, which allocated the execution of the most lucrative crafts and professions to the Spanish and the Creoles, leaving the rest to the Native Indians. The control of artistic production was assigned to civil servants known as *veedores* (that is, inspectors), who were in charge of destroying unorthodox works and ensuring that the Native Indians did not paint, sculpt or print sacred images. The Native Indians were prohibited from executing such works and were only allowed to paint landscapes, still lifes, produce decorative paintings, sculptures, pencil drawings, and, in exceptional cases, portraits. Once they extended beyond the scope of ornamentation in carved or painted objects, the Native Indians were forced to copy authorised European prints or paintings, which were provided to them by Spanish masters such as the *encomenderos*, *veedores* or Catholic priests. This is the origin of the tradition present even today on Olinalá boxes or other lacquered objects produced elsewhere, as well as the magnificent *pulquería* paintings of Mexican art that existed almost throughout the nineteenth century.[2] The production of religious images were reserved for the Spanish and the trusted Creoles; the survival of the tradition of indigenous Mexican art was feared and strong precautions were taken by authority figures against the plastic genius of Mexico. Nevertheless, although they succeeded in suppressing and conditioning the expression of this art for three centuries, they were not able to destroy it.

It is important to note that this situation had originated from the experiences in the dawn of the new order as early as the sixteenth century; the evangelist friars, who were the highly efficient assistants of military and civil conquerors, were extremely short of visual material to propagandise with images. Propaganda was crucially significant, as not only there was a problem of linguistic differences, but also a huge abyss between the two forms of writing: the Mexican language had an ideographic script expressed through images, whereas the Spanish language had a phonetic script expressed by signs. Thus, there was a great need for paintings, drawings, prints and sculptures that spoke a language everyone could understand. The friars sent the native artists they Christianised to Italy to study Catholic painting; however, when these artists returned from Italy, it became apparent that they had not been influenced by the pompous rhetoric and the exaggerated plastics that the Baroque followers of Michelangelo and Raphael used at the time. Instead, the native artists were inspired by pre-Giottescan or Giottescan painters of medieval Italy, a period in which the public fought against the feudal lords and the exploitive Popes. As parabolic examples, they were using scenes from the life of Christ, who reprimanded temple merchants and condemned the rich, whose entry into Paradise would be more difficult than a camel going through the eye of a needle.

The works of the Native Indians, who crossbred their art with the best features of the innovative and rebellious paintings of late medieval Italy, were simply magnificent. A proof of this can be found on the walls of Actopan, Epazoyucan, Huejotzingo, Tepeaca, and other places, where the early colonial architecture also yields the best examples under Spanish rule. The prevalent and evident kinship with the wonderful frescoes and codices of old cultures, as well as the new and implicit subversiveness undoubtedly connected to the works of the old masters, centred on the lives of the people who fought for their freedom, must have alerted the friars, doctors and judges who viewed the works of the Christianised Indians. Still, there was something more: when constructing the churches, the Native Indians had buried (surreptitiously, or under the dissimulation of the friar that needed good customers, as well as copious tithes and fees that were to be provided by the same Natives?) the old idols, the personifications of poetic-materialists of natural forces, and the indestructible human impulses behind and even under the altars.

Yet, something even more important took place: the 'Sun' and the 'Moon' flanking the crucifixes, the bouquets of flowers on the altars and under the curtains, and the images of water god Tláloc were evident in the paintings of the natives: they were integrated with the elements of the apparently Catholic elements in the painting. Made of maize cobs, the horizontal arm of the cross represents the earth, whereas the vertical arm represents the stream of water drops fertilising the earth; the four-armed cross, the four movements of the sun, the four equinoxes, the four corners of the firmament, the north, the south, the east and the west; the four elements, earth, water, air and fire; the first four men, red, yellow, black and white, created by the three serpents fledged with green quetzal feathers, before everything else, when the waters were on the brink of water as gas. Lord of the Flash of Lightning, Lord of the Thunder of Lighting, Lord of the Treads of Lightning; the tree people of our creator Trinity and the thunderbolt that unites them – together, all four constitute the basic motion power of matter and create all its forms. A few examples of these magnificent, occultist Christ-Tlálocs have been saved from the fervour of the *veedores* and survived to date.

The worship dance and prayer of the Native Mexicans in Catholic temples were and continue to be directed at these hidden images. This is why it was necessary to place the Sun and the Moon in a visible place in all the churches. Otherwise, the natives would not become members of the church and give alms or pay tithes.

Coupled with the necessity to construct a solid base for colonial domination by destroying the old culture when possible, all these reasons led the Spanish to establish laws, regulations, and the inspection system they used against the Mexican plastic genius. For this same reason, the emergence of an officially recognised native painter was approved in the eighteenth century by the exploitive, colonising society that happily consumed his production. This painter was Miguel Cabrera, whose indigenousness could only be discerned in his face and in his work – a simple distinction, which contained a feline elegance that was far different from the austere and sullen expression of the Spanish. Already filled with the light blues and pleasant pinks of the Catholics, the elegance of this native painter corresponded wonderfully with the intentions of the extremely intelligent and politicised Society of Jesus (or, the Jesuits). From the onset, as soon as the first clouds of a pending storm appeared in the horizon, the Society had clearly understood the danger it was about to encounter; during the gale of the bourgeois revolution with its militant French Masons, the Goddess of Wisdom, and the terrible battalions of *sans-culotte*, the Society of Jesus took advantage of the calming sensuality of mysticism that permeated the church like incense smoke, to prevent the ship of the church from being capsized in the waves. The sins could always be forgiven by means of gallant and devoted penance, so long as it was accompanied by personal and economic contributions – dictated by the holy court of penance – that would please the ministers and increase the capital of the church. Baroque art and literature were among the fundamental elements of this calming, holy incense; today in Mexico, we still suffer from the smell of this incense preserved in urns of all kinds.

Later, following the political independence that failed for lack of the necessary foundations of national economic independence, the post-feudalist sub-bourgeoisie of the old colony, which only managed to become a semi-colony after eleven years of struggle and sacrifice, tried to replace the Spanish masters and oppress the indigenous and undomesticated masses in a similar or worse manner. However, like all others, they failed at that attempt as well.

The social classes that ensued the Spanish domination failed due to the inherited historical ineptitude and biological incapacity.

The first reason was that the form of paternalistic feudal social regime that prevailed in the Spanish colonies was impervious to the movements arising in other European countries and to the Reformation, which supported the bourgeois revolution and its tremendous progressive power with its free assessment and liberalism.

The second reason was that the new masters had inherited a considerable part of the endless pathological treasures and booties that their illustrious conquering ancestors had collected during their 'heroic deeds' across the world. Hereditary syphilis and the subsequent state of mental illness included a long and extensive process of general paralysis; various neuroses caused by suppression and trauma as a result of the old education, in other words, the sexual oppression instigated by social, moral and religious prejudices, the oppression of all kinds of impulses required for the discipline to generate ruling classes, were all a result of the oldest collective mental sufferings, which were at the root of the Greco–Latin European slave culture.

Sociologically, the failure of the post-colonial social classes was due to their incapacity to rise to power as such. From post-feudalists to workers, all social classes demonstrated the same incapacity. Once a certain social class failed to rise to power, the only force that could exert control came to power: the armed political institution or the army-police. The army was under the command of militant politicians with or without uniform, yet all of them were armed; the only force able to maintain national unity in Mexico and in all the other semi-colonial Latin American countries like ours was the army. In all these countries, the power of the army always exists as the true single governmental authority behind the more or less civil and democratic-looking individuals or groups: despite all the defects it can and did have, that army is the only thing that has made possible the national existence of the Indian Americans of our continent after the separation of the metropolises.

Of course, the different nations that constitute Latin America, all of which are devoid of a national economy, have something in common: they have been controlled by more or less liberal and progressive governments, and even some greatly heroic ones as in case of Paraguay, the light of native Indian Americans, always in search of foreign masters. The progressive character of these governments in Mexico, and in some of the other countries in the south of Rio Bravo, has been determined by social phenomena and naturally reflected in culture. It is instigated by the needs of modern industrialisation and the interests of invested capital, and the inevitable increase in the living standard of the masses to create consumers for the industries established by the capital. That is to say, the driving force of that progressivism has been the advancement in the organisation capacity, and, consequently, the industrialised mentality of the workers and farmers, borne out of a social phenomenon.

With its continuously increasing dialectic contradictions, this phenomenon has indeed led to the resurgence and reappearance of the old Native American culture, which could not be destroyed by the archaic and backward colonialism established to sustain the dying feudalism in Europe and, in the ensuing years, by the inept semi-colonial sub-bourgeoisie in the pseudo-independent country. This self-preservation is one of the most valuable consequences produced by the dialectic contradictions on the balance sheet of Mexican history, benefitting the progressive segment of present-day Mexican people and all the inhabitants of the

American continent who want to march towards a much better social order in the future. If the people can work for this objective through the struggles of our time, then a unified and truly democratic America can be built.

Mexico's development through time and space is not rectilinear, simple and dry; it is more like an electric current – fast but sinuous, and full of sparks that diffuse into the atmosphere it traverses. The social and historical atmosphere of Mexico is highly complex due to the diversity of multiple elements that constitute it.

The modes of the country's social development are clearly read in the past and present examples of Mexican art. The more spontaneously and freely executed art in Mexico – namely the art of the people for the people – reveals with great clarity the two fundamental elements in its origin; however, these two elements coexist harmoniously without any external pressure and without mixing with or degenerating one another. This is evident in the devotional paintings or altar-pieces we call *retablo*. In these works, the Native American sense of plastic arts is conserved by a monumental realism that remains effective with smaller physical dimensions and the extraordinary colour use of the natives. On the other hand, the suspended mystical element in the atmosphere of the painting is accepted as an ornament of the sky and nothing else, whereas the occultist and poetic materialism governs the people, who believe that they benefit from Jesus and the Virgin Mary on earth, and by the miracle of the Spanish saints floating above the mystical clouds. The altarpieces are the best products of mysticism in semi-colonial Mexico throughout the nineteenth and in the early years of the twentieth century. During this period, José María Velasco was the most outstanding artist whose work was devoid of any Spanishness.

Towards 1921, symptoms began to appear in Mexican art that expressed the people's impulse to leave behind the semi-colonial state, regain their economic and political independence, and emerge with their own emancipated individuality on the world scene. All the Mexican paintings produced between 1921 and 1943 with some positive value reflect these symptoms like a mirror. As the dialectic opposite of the positive acquisition that modern Mexican painting represents, the plastic manifestations that continue to offer semi-colonial and subordinate character also coexist in this context; they are lamentable and provincial imitations of the art of the European metropolis. Unlike the artists in the United States and South America, who admirably affirm the independent existence of American art and culture, they are equivalent to the miserable by-products of North and South American artists afflicted with the same disease. The pseudo-artists who still suffer from the semi-colonialist endemic that transforms them into the footmen of Europe can be divided into two large groups:

a) Those that copy the inferior products of bourgeois and petit-bourgeois European art, painters of the images that adorn the postcards, calendars and commercial magazines sold at churches; tasteless portraits, 'paintings' that can only be seen in the homes of generals and the nouveau riche, and – even worse – the official portraits of the chiefs of state.

b) The more astute and well-informed, young and old suppliers of art galleries; academic painters who copied Murillo, Rafael, Ingres … or Clavé–Fabrés in San Carlos, are now replaced by new academic artists who copy Picasso, Chirico, Miró … or Dalí–Sert, again in San Carlos or a number of other places. There is no digestion without the excrement.

Amid the panorama of all Mexican painting of quality produced in the last twenty years, the paintings of Frida Kahlo Calderón shine like clear, hard, precious … diamonds in the centre of a great piece of jewellery. Jesus, Mary and the saints disappear from the altarpiece. Not just any miracle but the permanent miracle constitutes the subject of the painting: the vitality, always flowing, always different, and always the same in its circulation through the veins and the sidereal bodies. A life contains the elements of all the lives and if one penetrates all the way to the bottom, one encounters LIFE's abysmal depth, vertiginous height, and infinite ramifications weaved for centuries of light and shadow. For this reason, Frida's altarpieces always portray her own life. Two Fridas, both equal to, yet different from one another.

The analytical, constructive-destructive, and deluded sceptic German – the genes of her father – prevails, completely eradicating the Spanish and allying with the Native Indian – the genes of her mother. Beyond the wide open door of the sky, there is only an implacable and marvellous space, where the Sun and the Moon shine together over the pyramids; despite their microscopic size for a star and a planet, they have an astounding greatness and an immense system of proportions that echo the entire universe. The toy plane of the girl seated in the centre of the world equals imagination-mind in speed, much faster than the speed of light; she recognises the stars and the cities before reaching them by telescope or locomotives. It is a speed that resides in Frida, alone in the mechanised space, stretched out on a bed, from where she sees, crying, that the life-foetus is a flower-machine, a slow snail, a mannequin and bony armour in appearance, but in reality, an imagination-mind that travels faster than light.

A recurrent auto-portrait, not one of which resembles the other and looks more like Frida every time, changeable and permanent like the universal dialectic. The monumental realism is resplendent; occultist materialism in the heart cut in two, blood flowing from the tables, bathtubs, plants, flowers, and the arteries closed by the haemostatic forceps of the artist.

The monumental realism is expressed in its smallest dimension; tiny heads are almost sculpted as though they were colossal in size and thus appear as such when a magic projector amplifies them to the size of an entire wall. When Frida's visual background is put under the microscope, the mind appears; the network of veins and cells are different, requiring new elements such that the total capital of the art of painting is increased with a new perception.

Frida's altarpieces resemble neither other altarpieces, nor other painters, nor anything else. Frida's art is collectively individual, so monumentally realistic that in its total space, it is N-dimensional, mathematically speaking. Consequently, she paints the exterior, the interior and the background of herself and the world at the same time. In the oxygen plus hydrogen plus carbon sky, comprising electricity, the spirits of space Hurakán, Kukulkán and Gukamatz are alone with her parents and grandparents, and she is on earth and in the matter with thunder, lightning and thunderbolt that create man through their dialogues. For Frida, the mother figure is the tangible, the centre of everything, the matrix; sea, storm, nebula, woman.

Frida is the only example in the history of art of someone who tears open her heart and breast to tell the biological truth about what she feels in them. She painted her mother and her wet-nurse, aware that she did not really know their faces; the nutritive nana's face is only a hard stone Indian mask, and her nipples drip milk like rain fertilising the earth and tears fertilising pleasure. Her mother's face is Virgin Mary of Sorrows (Mater Dolorosa) with seven daggers of pain making possible the tear through which baby Frida emerges; the only human force which, starting with the extraordinary Aztec master who sculpted black basalt, moulded birth in its own true action.

A birth that produced the only woman, who has expressed in her work of art the feelings, functions and creative power of a woman with insurmountable KALIS-TEKNIKA.*

A birth that produced the painter, who is the greatest painter and the best testimony to the reality of the Renaissance of Mexican art.

Extract from Diego Rivera, 'Frida Kahlo and Mexican art', *Frida Kahlo and Diego Rivera from the Gelman Collection*, Pera Müzesi, Istanbul, 2011, p 62–72, first published in the *Bulletin of Mexican Seminary of Culture* by the Ministry of Education, October 1943.

1. *Encomienda* was a labour system mainly used by the Spanish crown during the colonisation of the America. The *encomenderos* were often comprised of conquistadors and soldiers, but also included women and native notables.

2. A public bar or tavern serving the Mexican drink *pulque*.

* Editor's note: references to non-Western belief systems can be found in numerous paintings and writings by Frida Kahlo. 'Kalis-teknika' alludes to Kali, the Hindu goddess of empowerment, and is possibly used by Rivera to ascribe to Kahlo the goddess's abilities.

Frida Kahlo *The miscarriage* 1932 (detail)

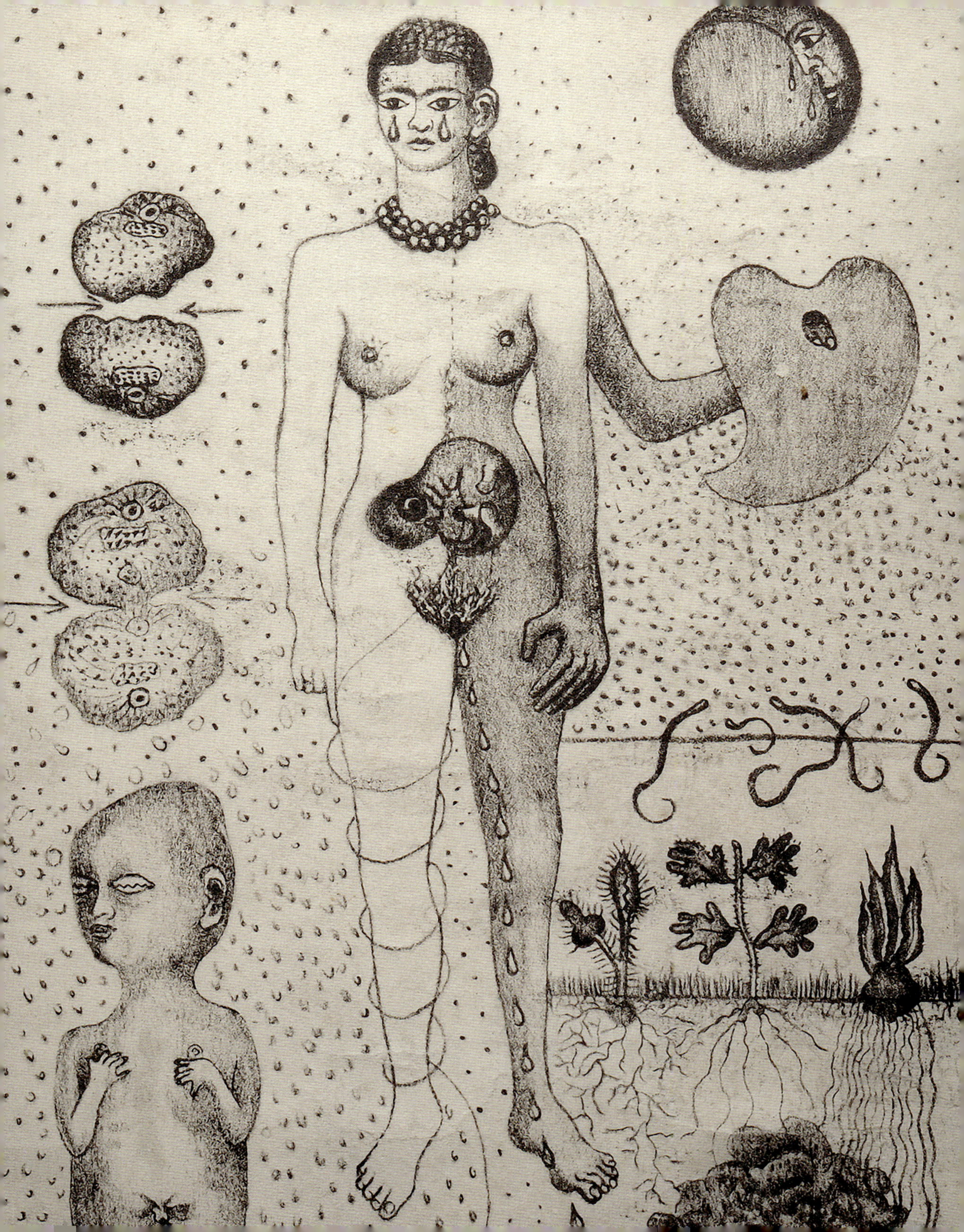

FRIDA KAHLO

–

Self-portrait with bed (Me and my doll)

1937

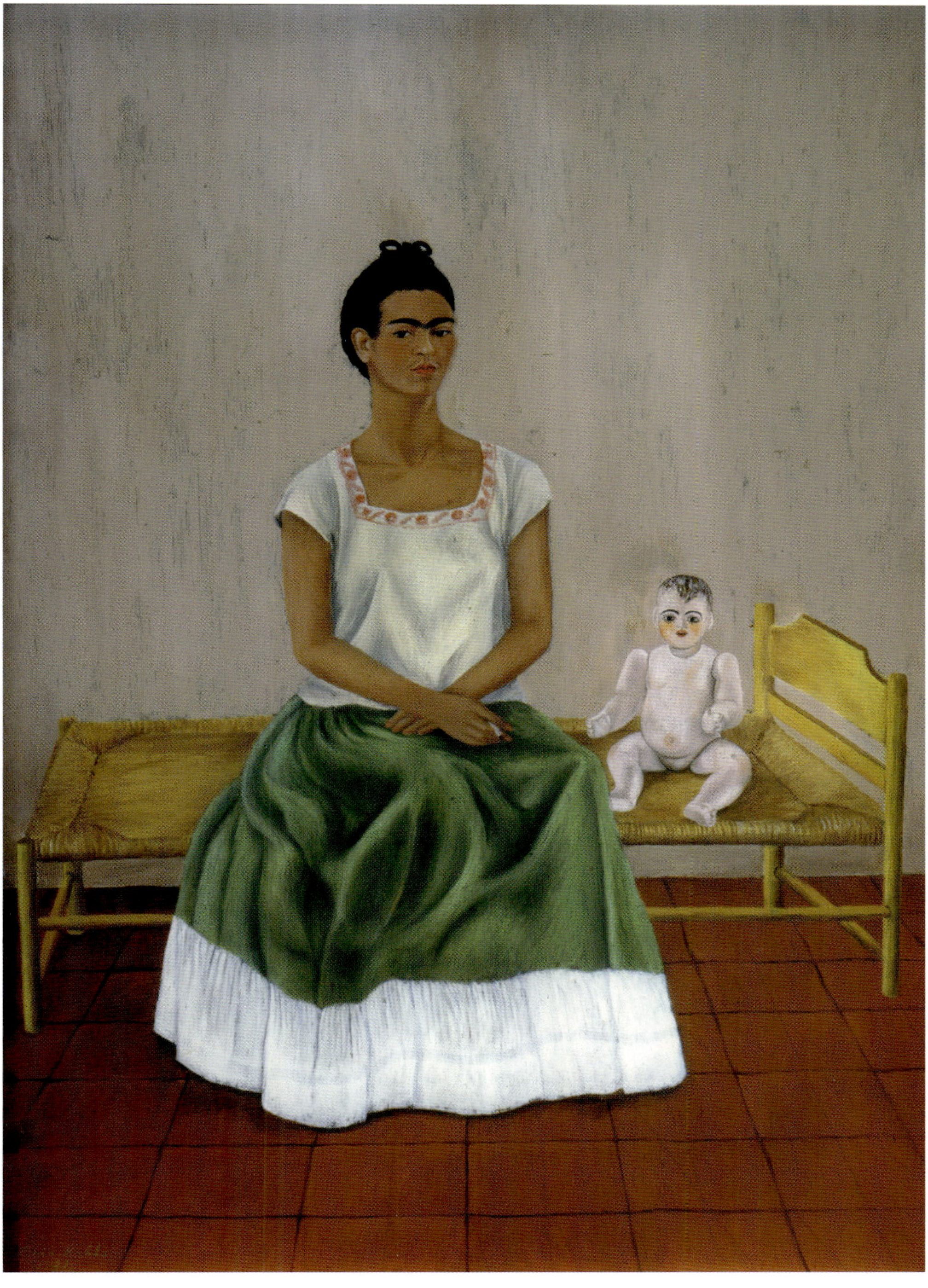

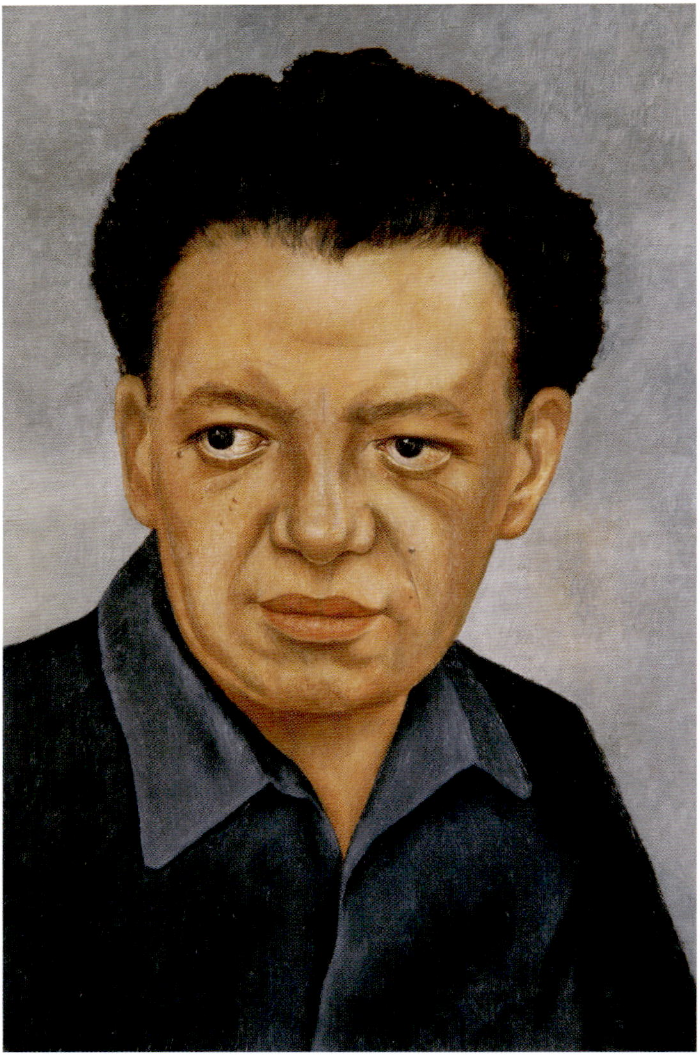

FRIDA KAHLO

–

Portrait of Diego Rivera

1937

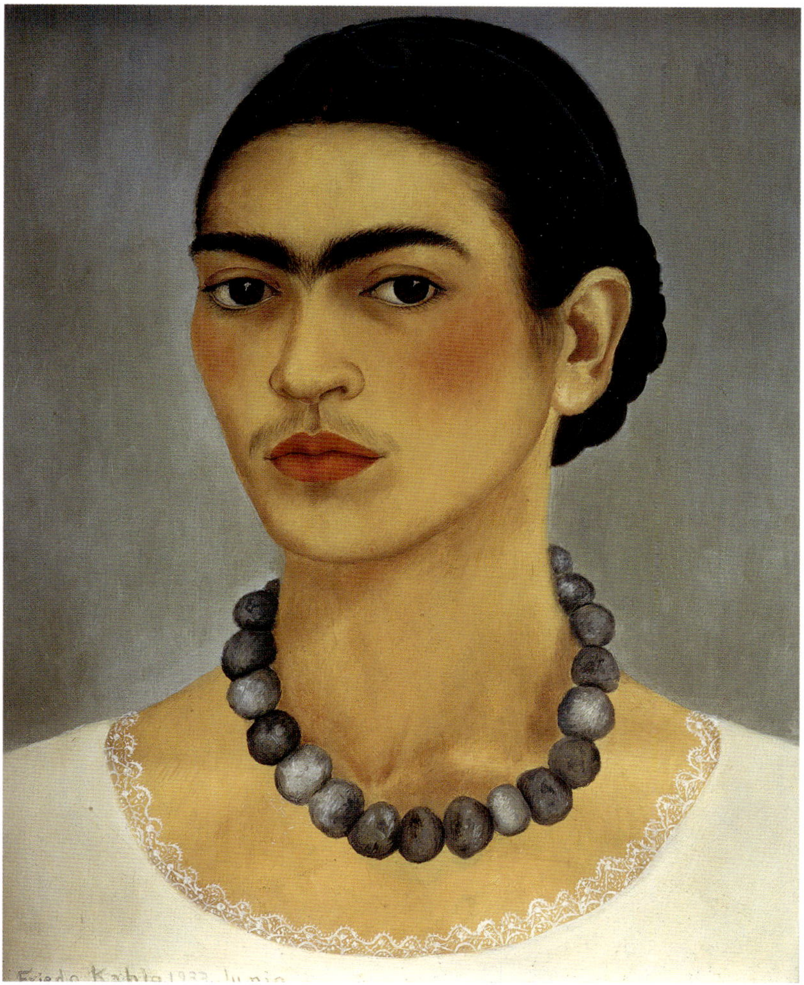

FRIDA KAHLO

–

Self-portrait with necklace

1933

FRIDA KAHLO

–

Self-portrait
with red and gold dress

1941

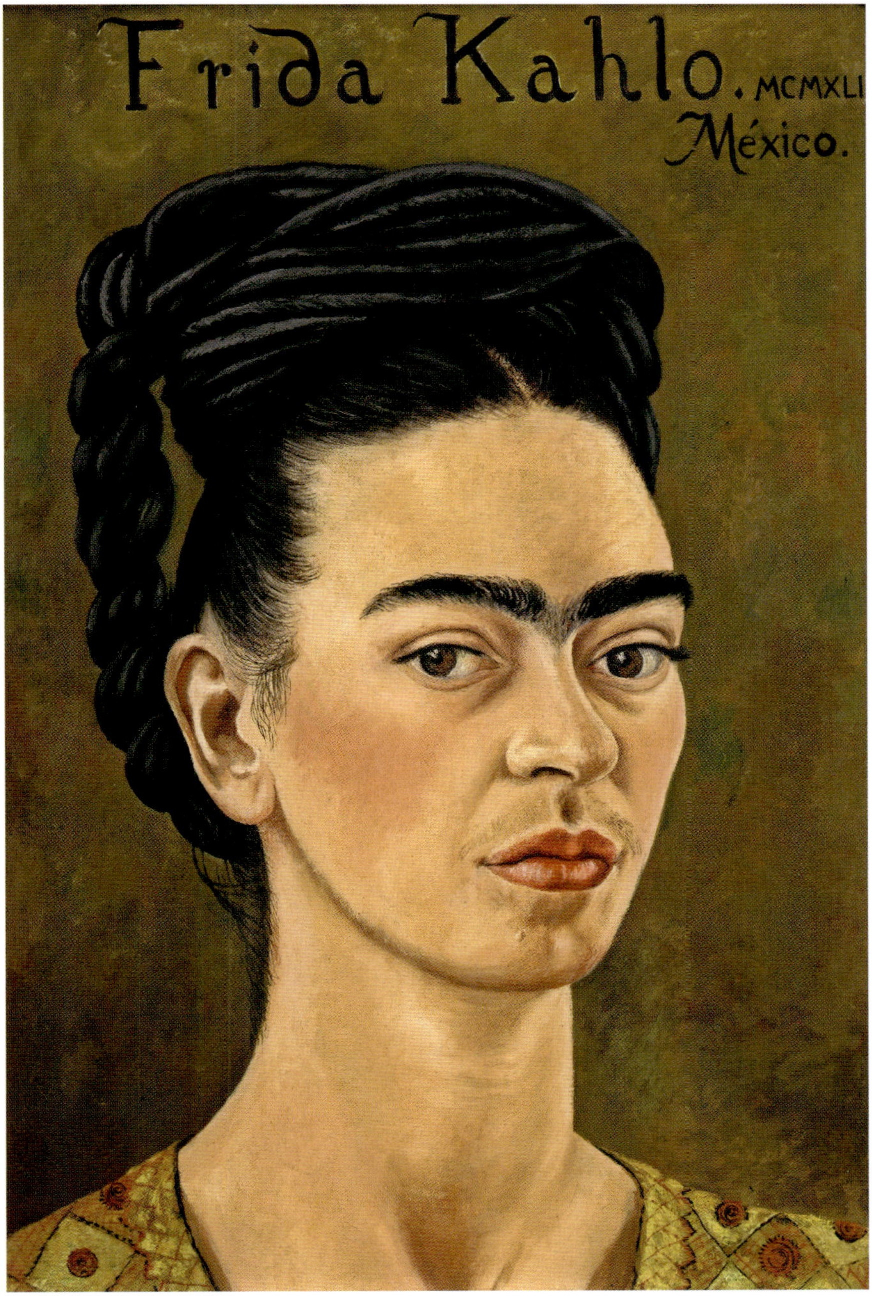
Frida Kahlo. MCMXLI
México.

FRIDA KAHLO

–

Self-portrait with braid

1941

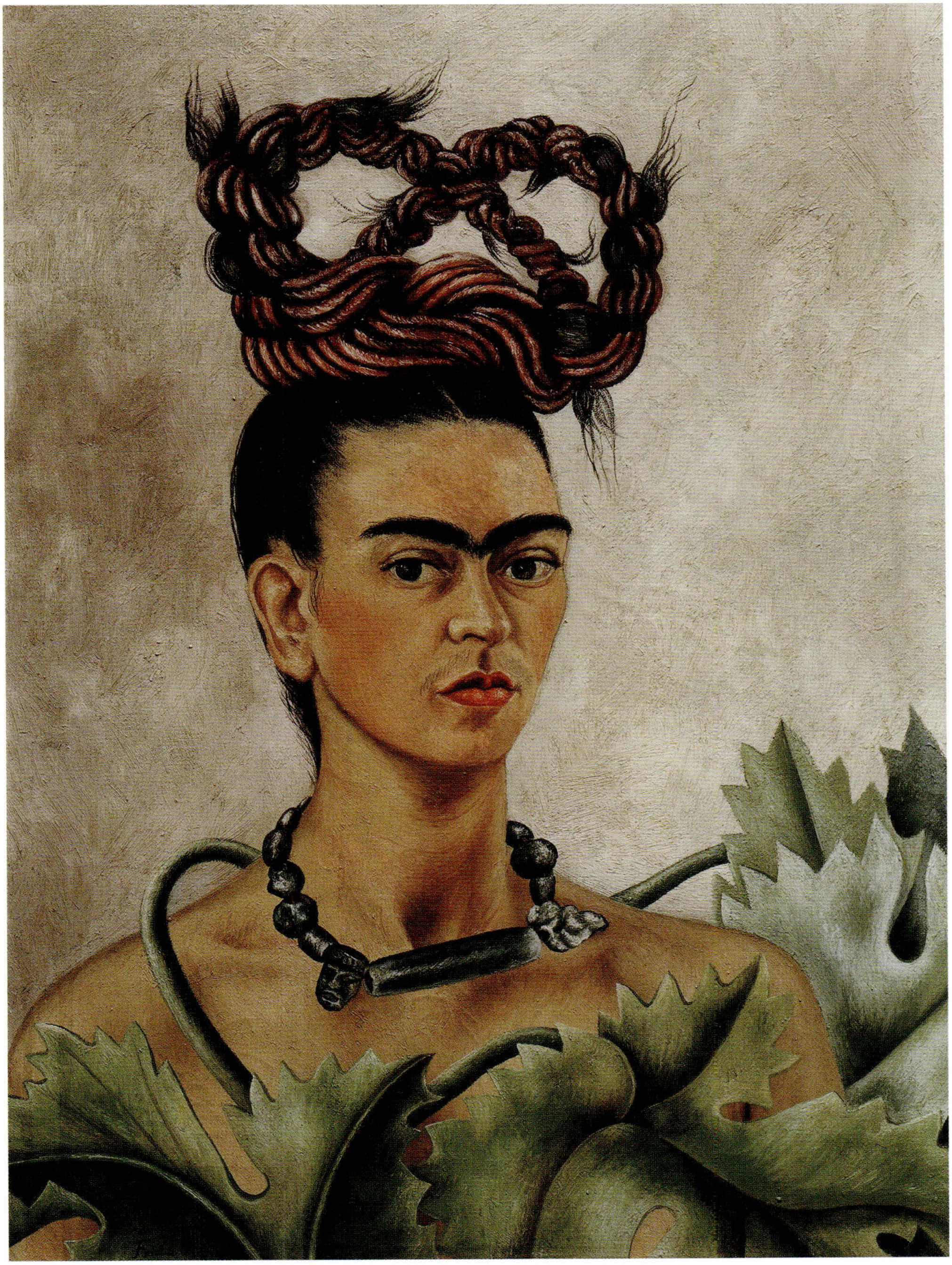

FRIDA KAHLO

–

Self-portrait with monkeys

1943

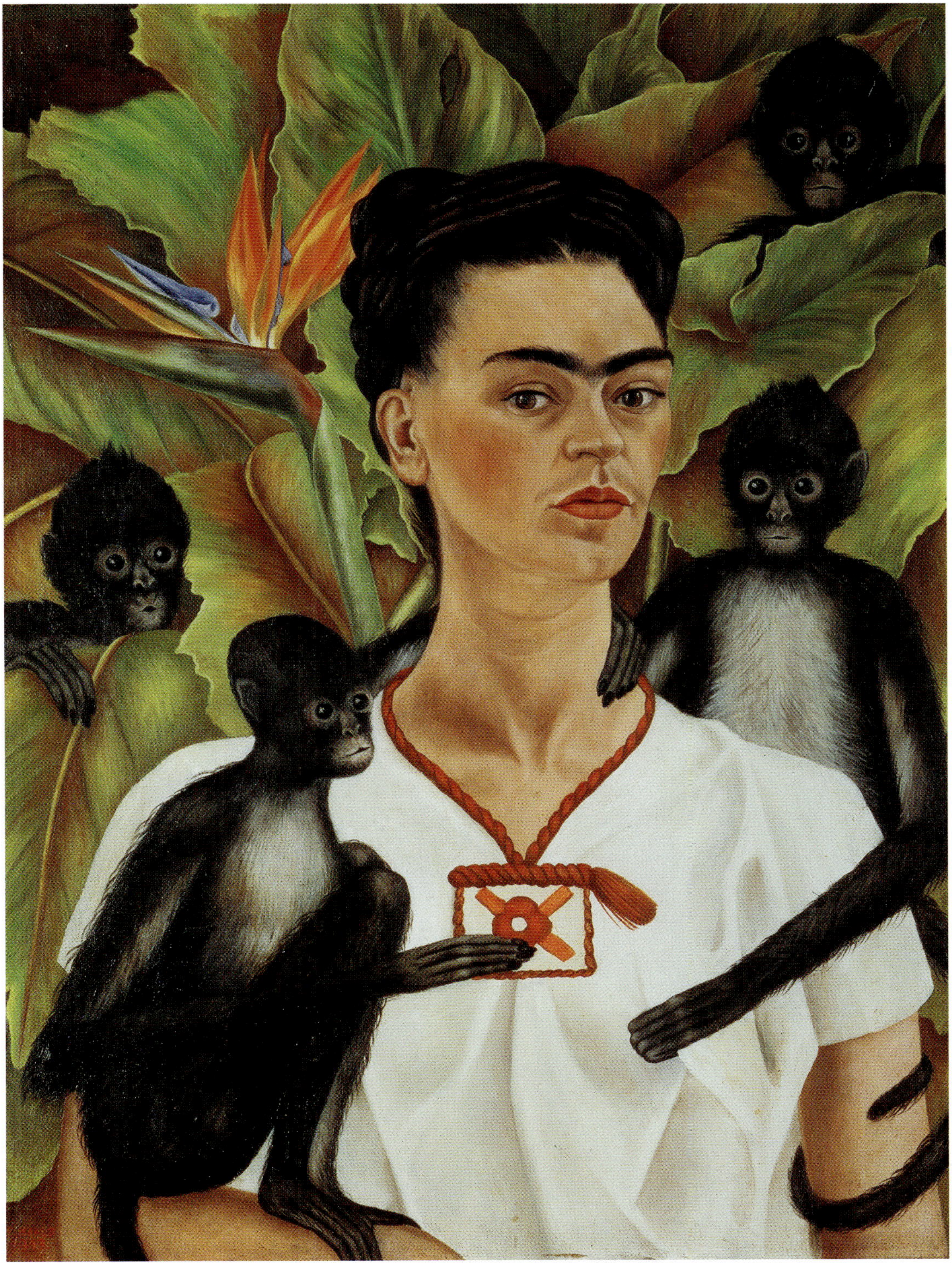

FRIDA KAHLO

–

Diego on my mind
(Self-portrait as Tehuana)

1943

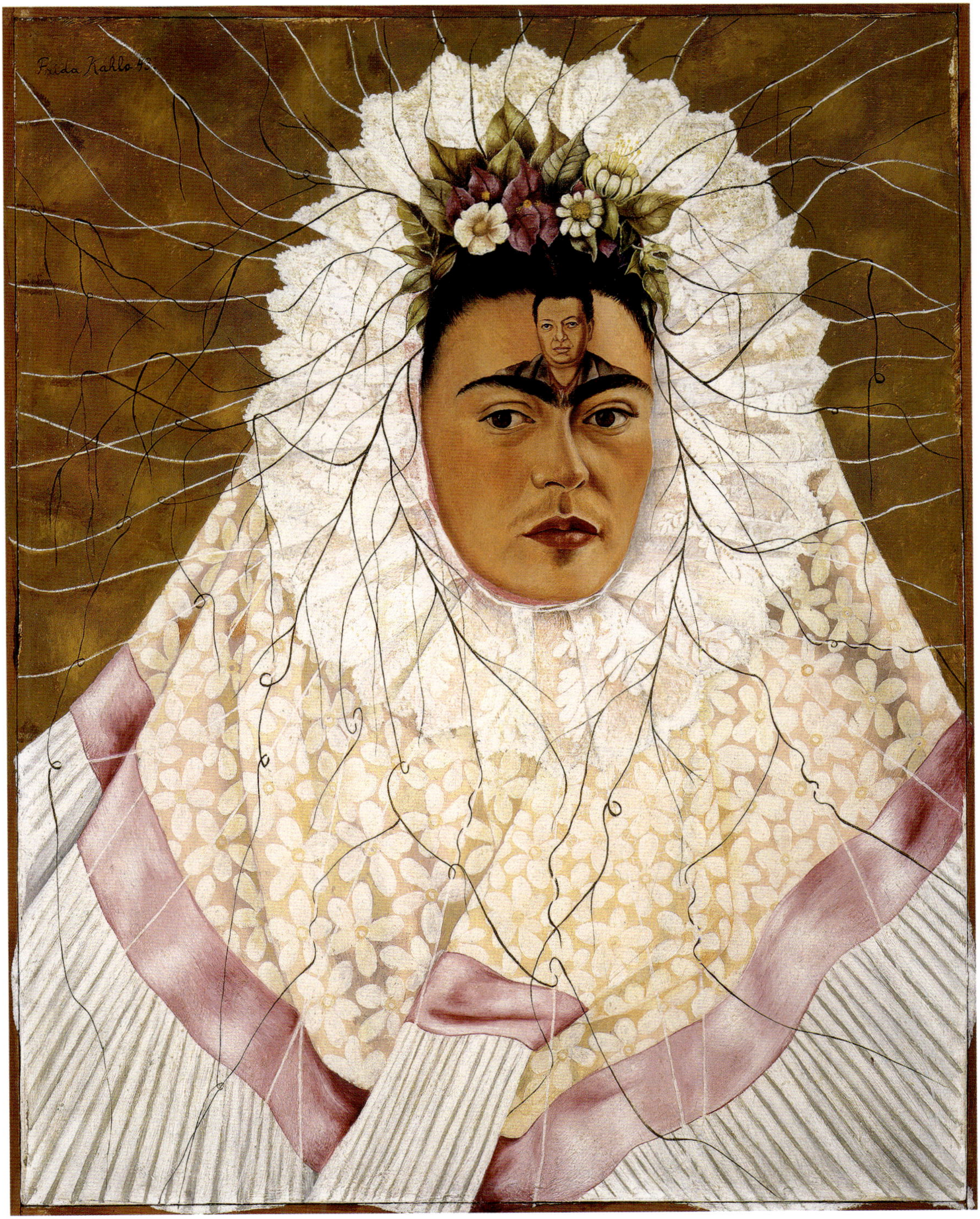
Frida Kahlo 43

FRIDA KAHLO

–

Portrait of Natasha Gelman

1943

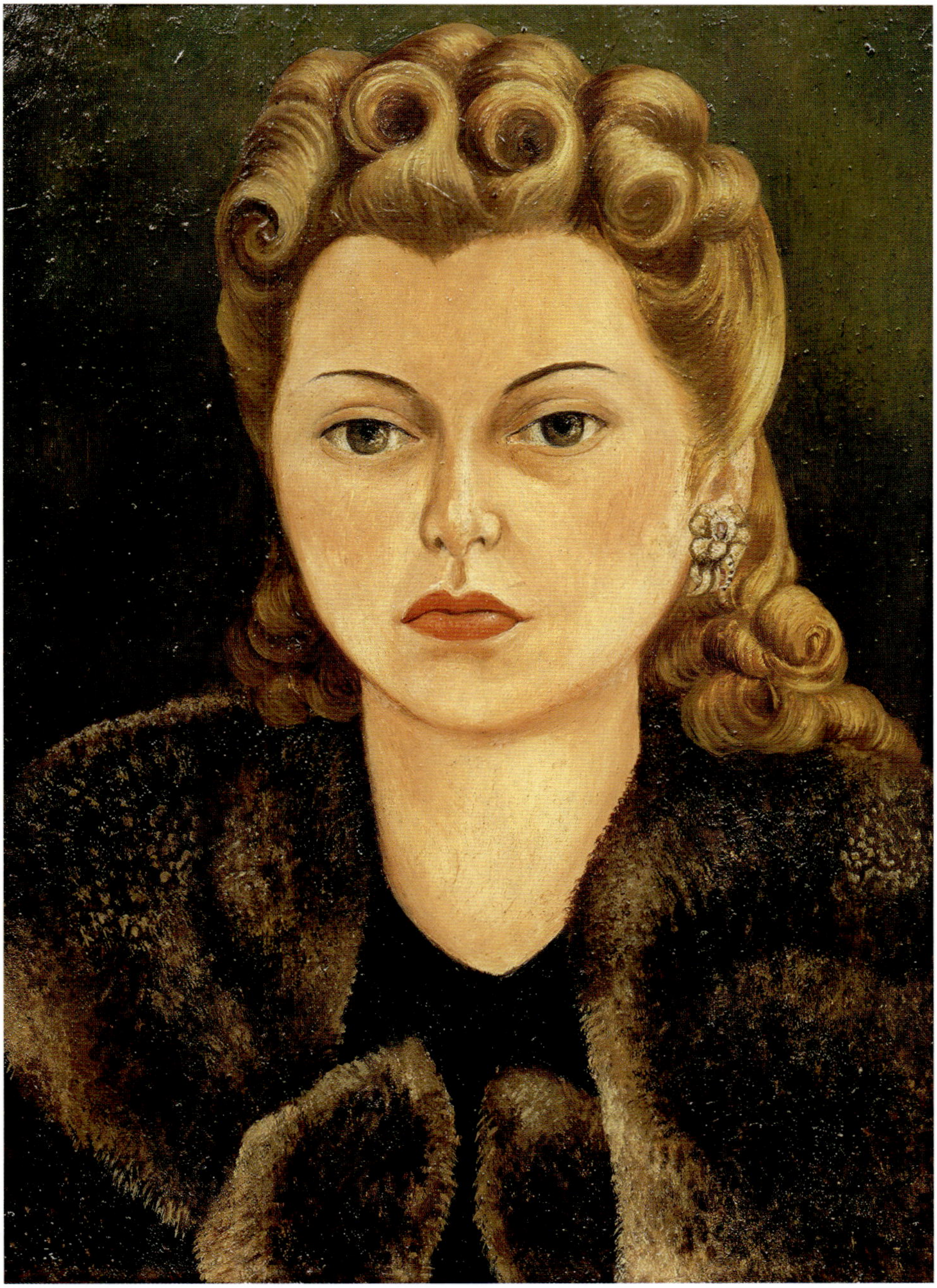

FRIDA KAHLO

–

The bride who
becomes frightened
when she sees
life opened

1943

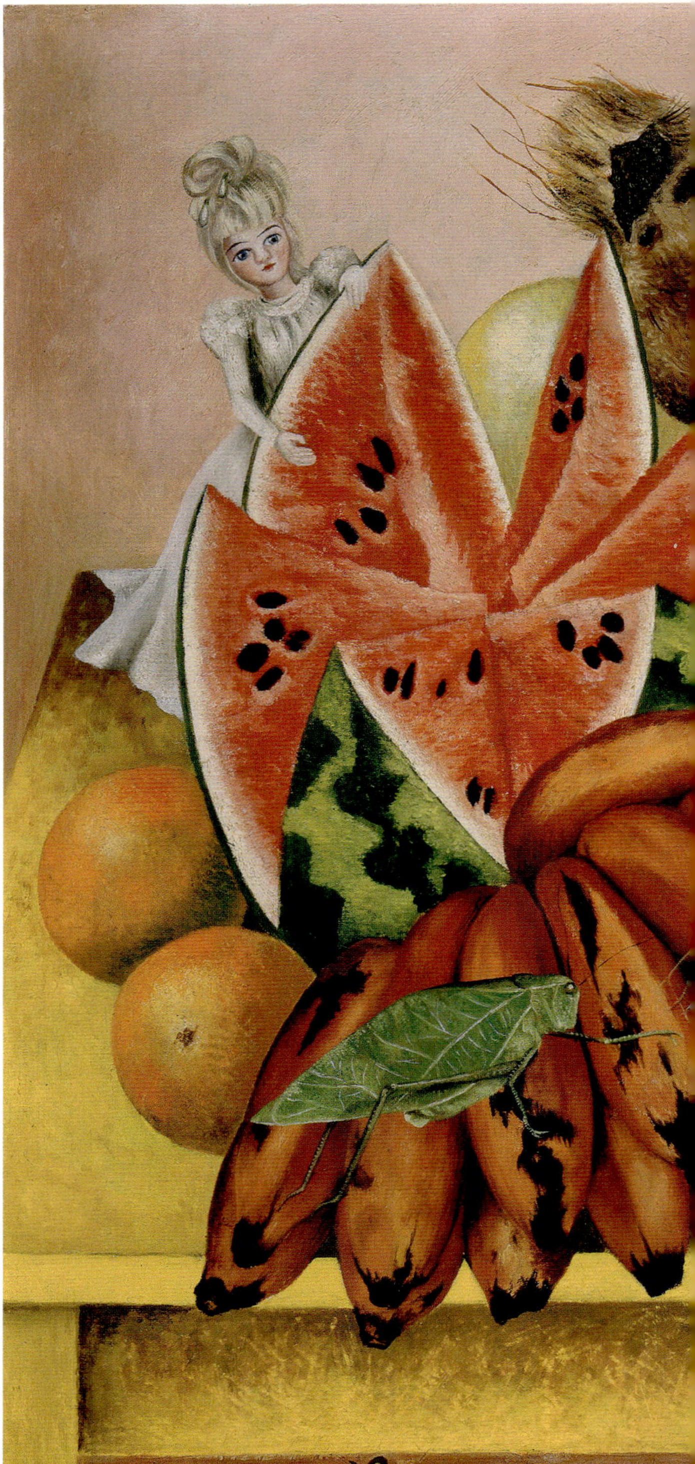

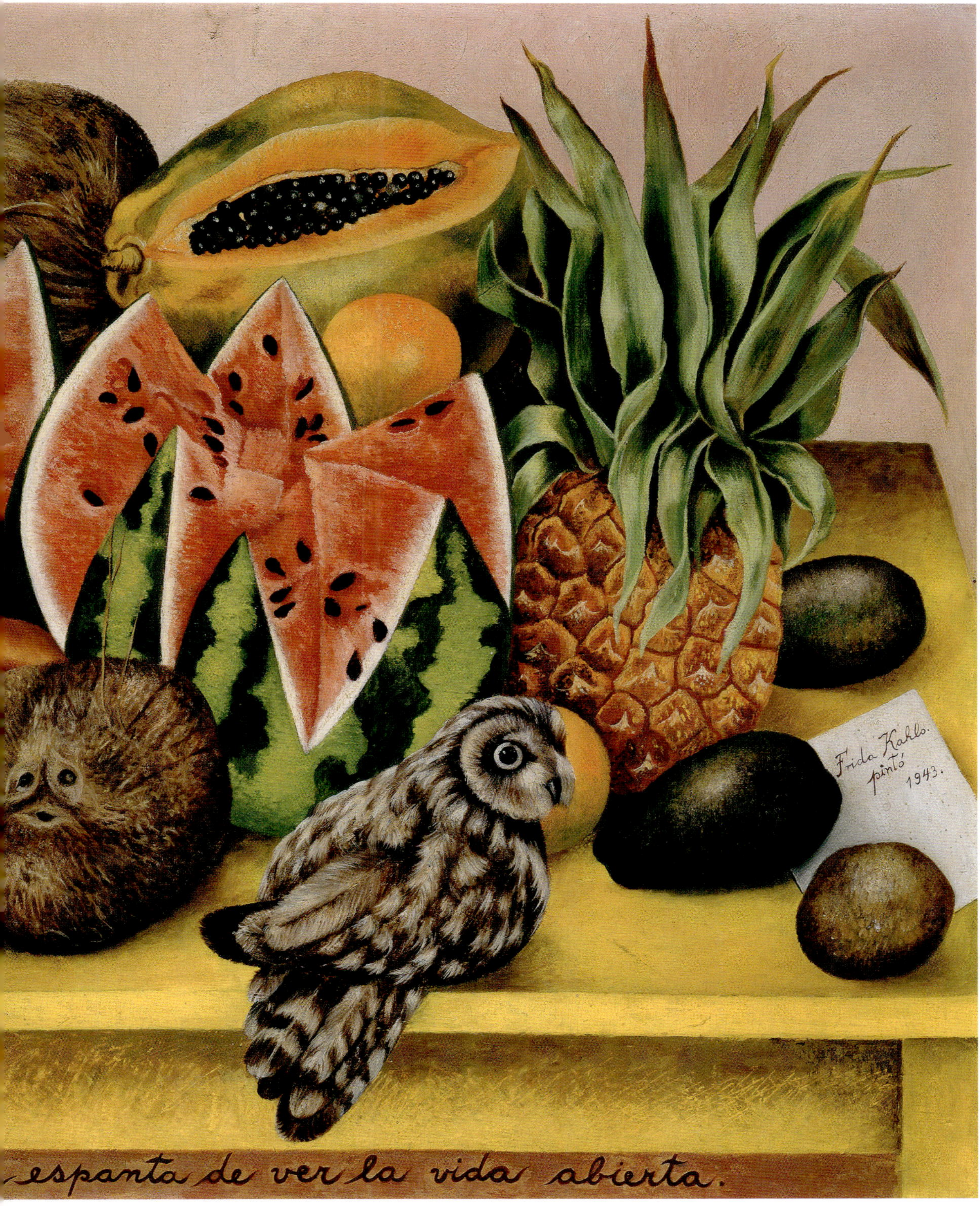
Frida Kahlo.
pintó
1943.
espanta de ver la vida abierta.

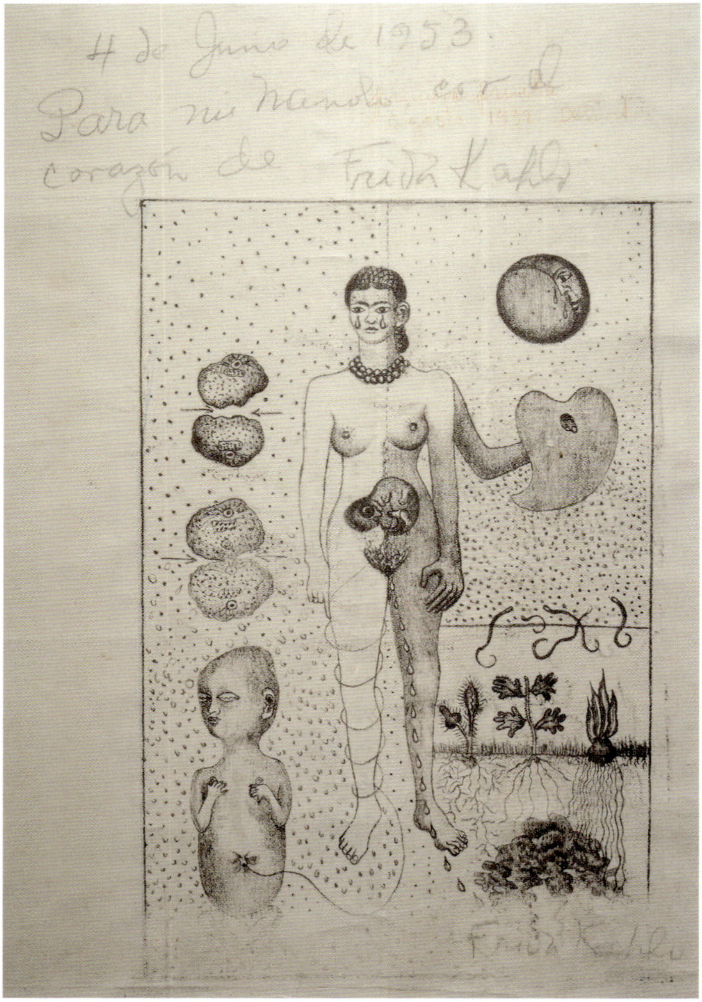

FRIDA KAHLO

–

left

The miscarriage 1932

–

opposite
clockwise fom top left

The sun peeks through the window 1932

Lady Liberty (Workers of the world unite) c1945

Untitled (Atomic bomb) c1951

Liberty c1946

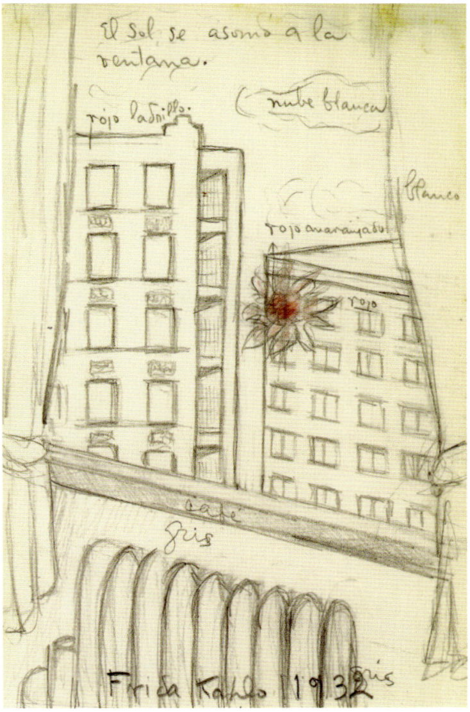
El Sol se asomó a la ventana.
rojo ladrillo.
nube blanca
blanco
rojo anaranjado
rojo
café
gris
Frida Kahlo 1932
gris

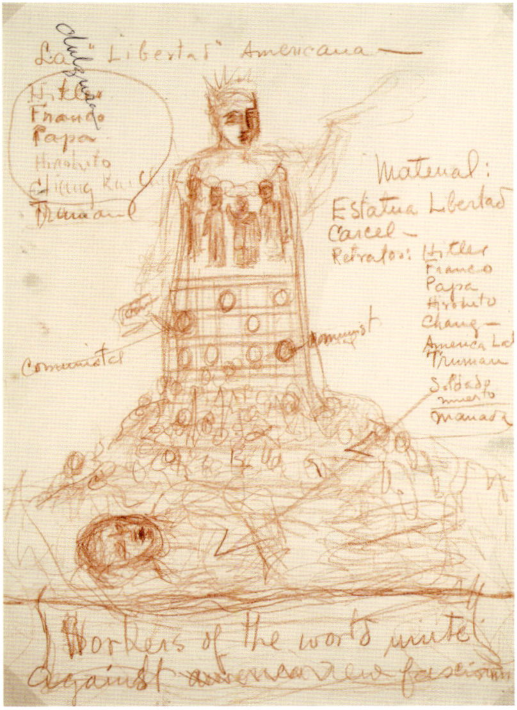
La "Libertad" Americana
Hitler
Franco
Papa
Hirohito
Truman
Material:
Estatua Libertad
Carcel
Retratos: Hitler
Franco
Papa
Hirohito
America Lat.
Truman
Workers of the world unite

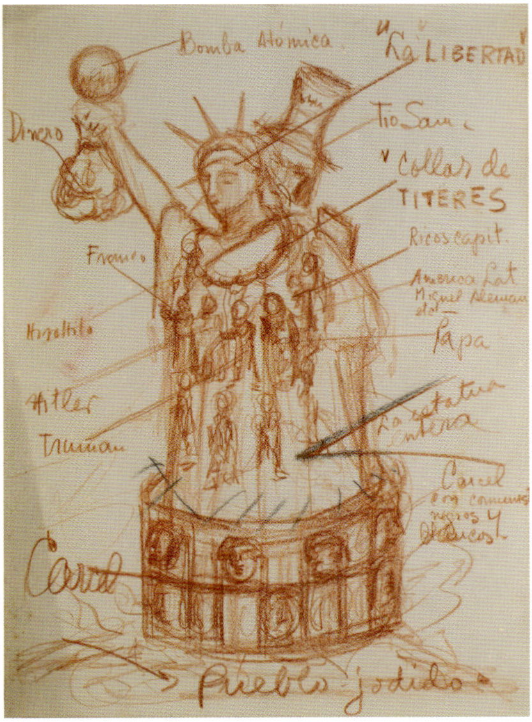
Bomba Atómica
"La LIBERTAD"
Dinero
Tío Sam
Collar de TITERES
Ricos capit.
Franco
America Lat.
Miguel Aleman
Hirohito
Papa
Hitler
La estatua entera
Truman
Carcel
Carcel
Pueblo jodido

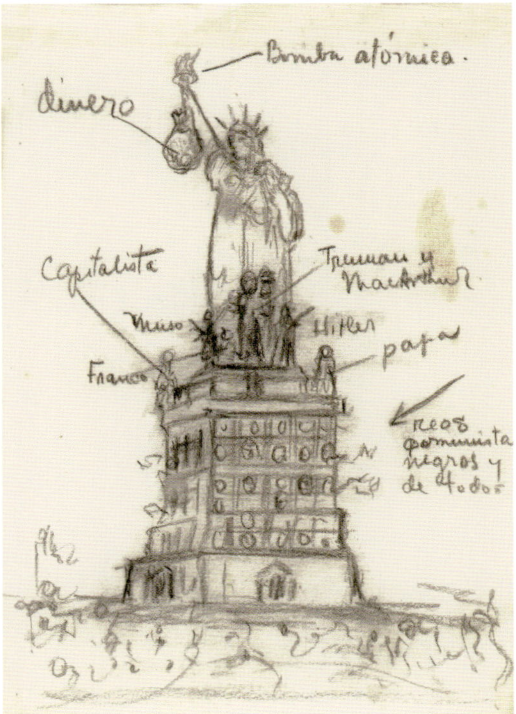
Bomba atómica.
dinero
Capitalista
Truman y MacArthur
Hitler
papa
Franco
reos comunista negros y de todos

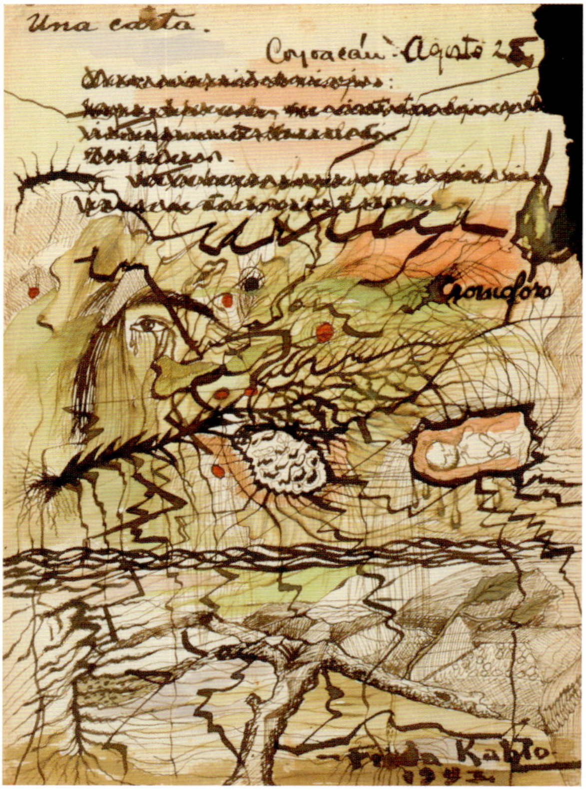

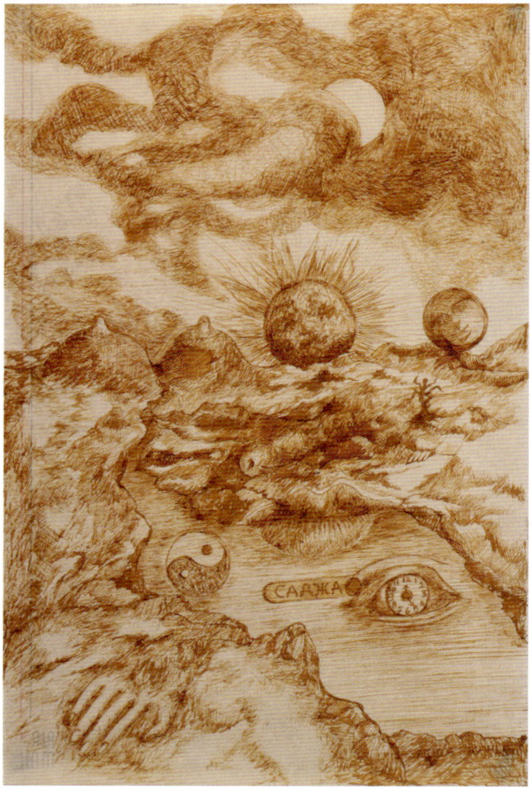

FRIDA KAHLO

–

from left

A brief 1943

11:25 (Carma III) 1946

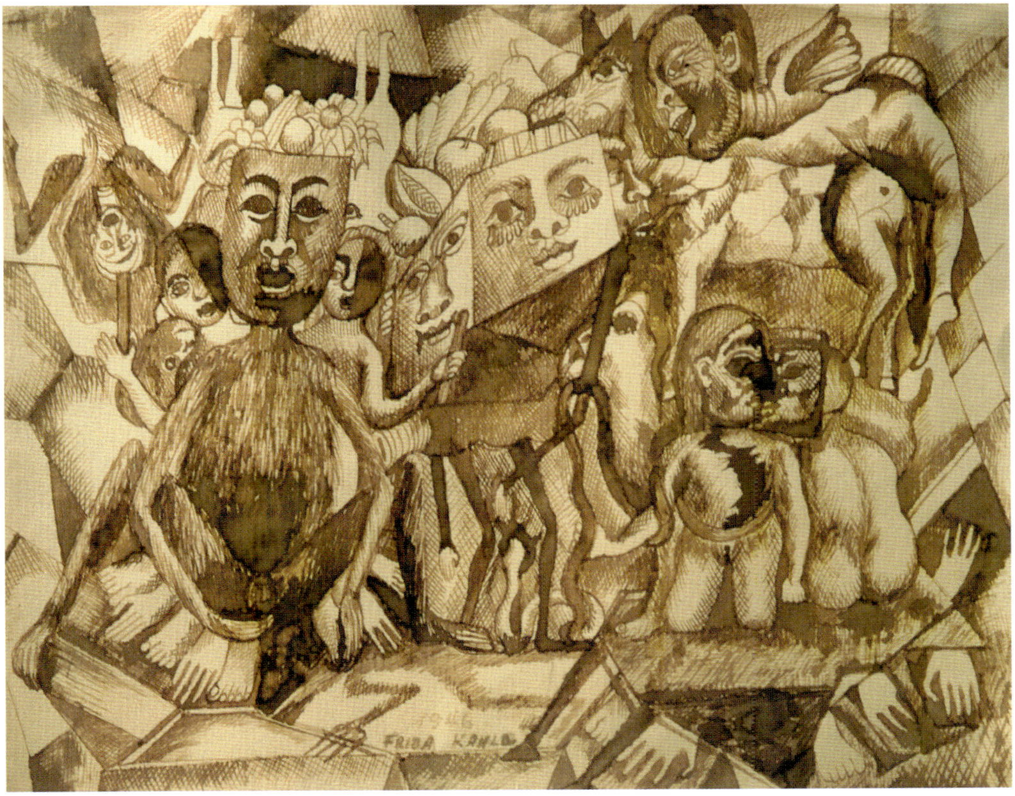

FRIDA KAHLO

—

Masks (Carma I)

1946

FRIDA KAHLO

–

The love embrace of the universe, the Earth (Mexico), Diego, me and Señor Xólotl

1949

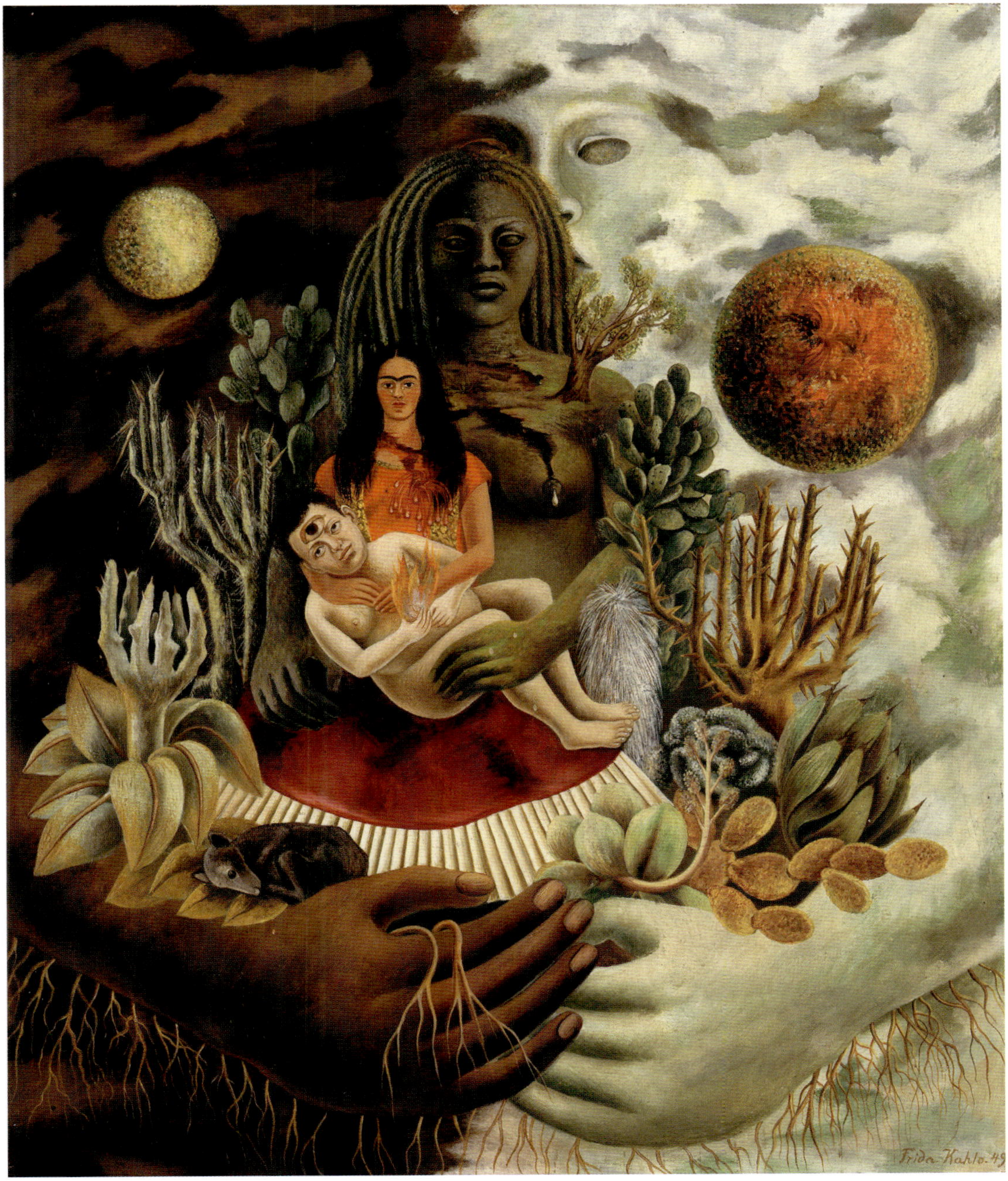
Frida Kahlo 49

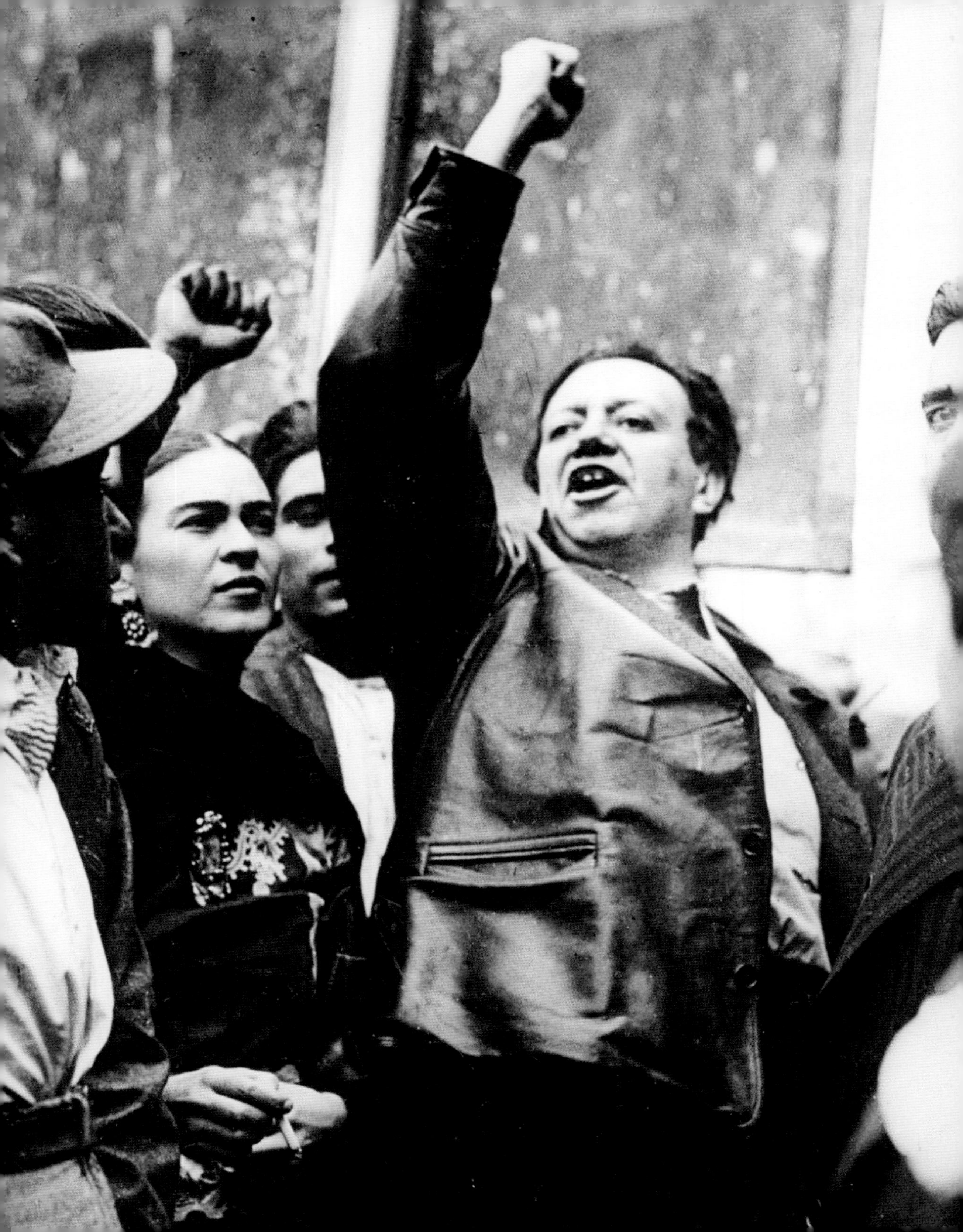

Diego

Frida and Diego during a Mexican
Labor anti-fascist demonstration
in Mexico City 1936
Photographer unknown

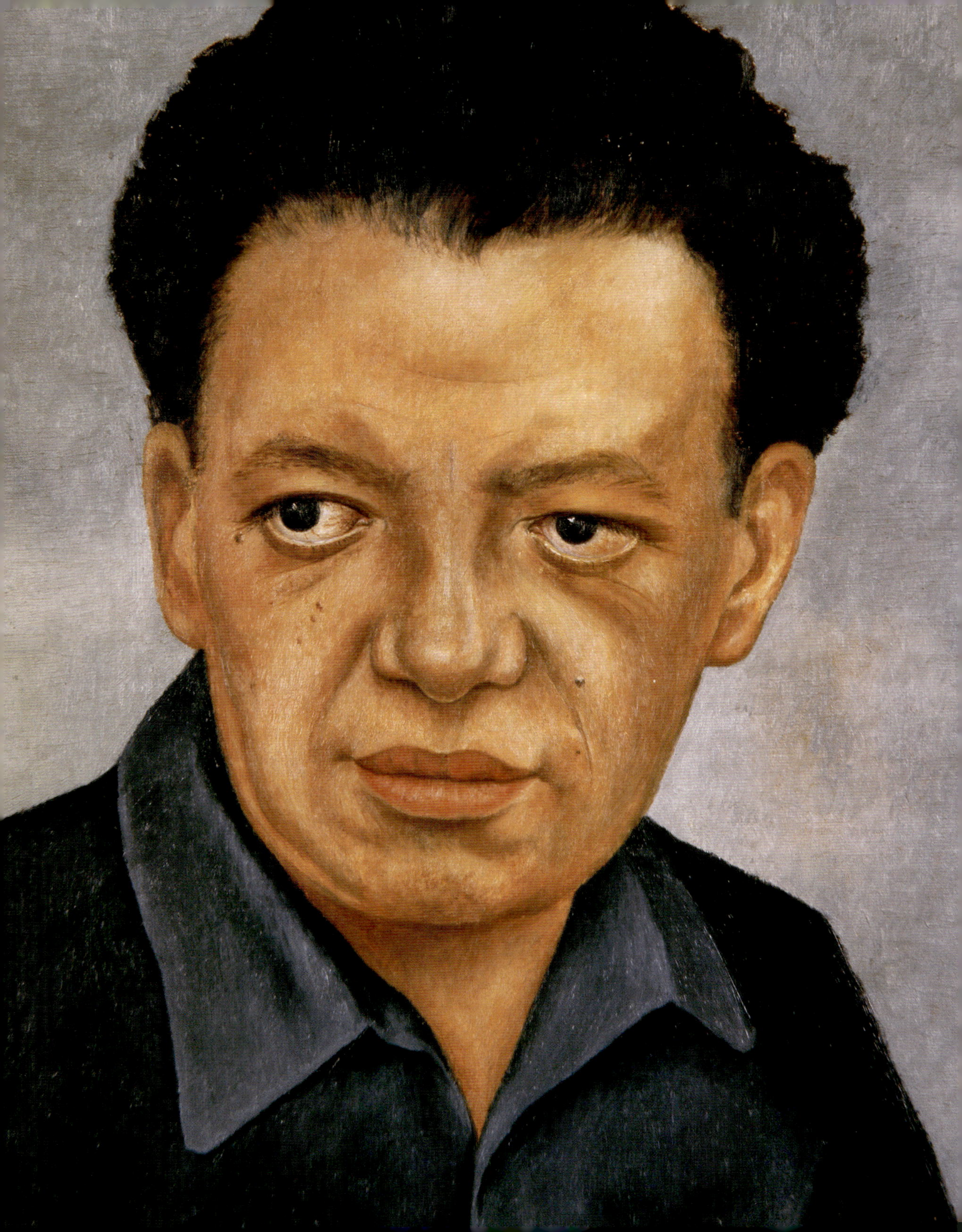

Portrait of Diego

–

BY FRIDA KAHLO

–

I must warn that this portrait of Diego will be painted in colours I am unfamiliar with: in words, and it will be the poorer for that; besides, I love Diego in such a way that I cannot be a 'spectator' of his life, but rather a part of it, so that – perhaps – I will exaggerate the positive aspects of his unique personality by trying to soften what could, even remotely, wound him.

This will not be a biographical account: I consider it more sincere to write only of the Diego I believe I have come to know a little in these twenty years I have lived near him. I will not speak of Diego as 'my husband', because that would be ridiculous; Diego has never been, nor will he ever be, anyone's 'husband'. Nor as my lover, for he embraces much beyond sexual limitations, and if I spoke of him as of a child, I would only describe or paint my own emotion, almost my self-portrait, not that of Diego. With this warning, and with the utmost clarity, I will try to speak the only truth: my own, in order to trace an outline, within my powers, of his image.

HIS FORM: with his Asiatic head and dark hair, so thin and fine that it seems to float in the air, Diego is an immense, enormous child, with a friendly face and a rather sad gaze. His large protuberant eyes, dark and extremely intelligent, are barely restrained – almost leaping from their orbits – by the swollen, bulging batrachian eyelids, and are set far apart from one another, more so than other eyes. They permit his gaze to embrace a wider visual field, as if they were constructed specially for a painter of spaces and multitudes. Between these eyes, one so far from the other, can be glimpsed the invisibility of Oriental wisdom, and but very seldom does there disappear from his full-lipped Buddha-like mouth a tender and ironic smile, the flower of his image.

Seeing him nude one thinks immediately of a frog child standing on its hind legs. His skin is greenish-white, like that of an aquatic animal. Only his hands and face are darker, burned by the sun. His narrow, rounded, infantile shoulders continue down without angles into feminine arms and end in marvellous, small, finely drawn hands, sensitive and subtle as antennas that communicate with the entire

Frida Kahlo *Portrait of Diego Rivera* 1937 (detail)

universe. It is astonishing that these hands have served to paint so much and still work indefatigably.

Of his chest it must be said: if he had disembarked on the island governed by Sappho, he would not have been executed by her warriors. The sensitivity of his marvellous breasts would have gained him admittance. Though his virility, specific and singular, also makes him desirable in dominions of empresses avid for masculine love.

His belly, enormous, smooth and tender as a sphere, rests on strong legs, as beautiful as columns, that end in large feet, splayed outward at an obtuse angle as if to embrace the whole earth and stand upon it without contradiction, like an antediluvian being, from which might emerge, from the waist up, an example of future humanity, two or three thousand years distant from us.

He sleeps in the foetal position and during his sleep he moves with elegant slowness, as if he were living in a liquid element. For his sensibility, expressed in his movements, it would seem that air is denser than water.

Diego's form is that of an affectionate monster, which the grandmother, the Ancient Concealer, the necessary and eternal matter, the mother of men, and all the gods invented by them in their delirium, out of fear and hunger, THE WOMAN, and among all of them – I MYSELF – would like always to hold in her arms like a newborn child.

HIS CONTENT: Diego exists to one side of all personal, limited and precise relations. Contradictory like everything that moves life, he is at once an immense caress and a violent discharge of powerful and unique forces.

He is experienced within himself, like the seed treasured up in the earth, and without, like the landscapes. Probably some of you expect a very personal, 'feminine' portrait of Diego from me, anecdotal, entertaining, full of complaints and a certain amount of gossip, of that 'decent' gossip that can be interpreted and used in accordance with the morbidity of each reader. Perhaps you expect to hear laments from me of 'how much one suffers' living with a man like Diego. But I don't believe the banks of a river suffer from letting it flow between them, nor that the earth suffers because it rains, nor that the atom suffers releasing its energy … for me, everything has a natural compensation. In my role, difficult and obscure, as ally to an extraordinary being, I enjoy the reward of a spot of green in a mass of red: the reward of equilibrium. The sorrows and joys that regulate life in this lie-infested society in which I live are not my sorrows and joys. If I have prejudices and am wounded by the actions of others, even those of Diego Rivera, I accept responsibility for my inability to see clearly, and if I don't have them, I have to accept that it is natural for red blood cells to fight against white ones without the slightest prejudice and that this phenomenon only signifies health. I will not be the one to undervalue Diego's fantastic personality, which I deeply respect, by saying stupid things about his life. I would like, on the contrary, to express as it deserves to be expressed, with the poetry I do not possess, what Diego really is.

Of his painting, his painting itself speaks – prodigiously enough.

I will leave it to the men of science to speak of his function as a human organism. Of his valuable social and revolutionary contribution, his objective and personal work, all those who know how to measure its incalculable importance in time may speak; but I, who have watched him live for twenty years, do not have the means to organise and describe the living images that might faintly, but deeply, trace the most basic lines of his figure. My ineptness can only produce a few opinions and they will be the only material I can offer.

The profound roots, the external influences and true causes that condition Diego's matchless personality are so vast and complex that my observations will be but small shoots on the many branches of the gigantic tree that is Diego.

There are three principal lines or directions I consider basic in his portrait: the first, that of being a constant, dynamic, extraordinarily sensitive and vital revolutionary combatant; an indefatigable worker at his trade, which he knows as few painters in the world do; a fantastic enthusiast for life and, at the same time, ever unsatisfied with not having succeeded in knowing more, building more and painting more. The second, that of being eternally curious, a tireless student of everything; and the third, his absolute lack of prejudices and, as a result, of faith, because Diego accepts – as Montaigne did – that 'where doubt ends, stupidity begins', and that whoever has faith in something admits his unconditional submission, without the freedom to analyse or to vary the course of events.
As a result of this utterly clear concept of reality, Diego is a rebel, and knowing so marvellously the materialist dialectic of life, Diego is a revolutionary. From this triangle, upon which the other modalities of Diego are erected, there emanates a sort of atmosphere that envelopes the whole. This mobile atmosphere is love, but love as a general structure, a movement that constructs beauty. I imagine that the world he would like to live in would be a great fiesta in which each and every being took part, from men to stones, suns and shadows: all cooperating with their own beauty and creative power. A fiesta of form, of colour, of movement, of sound, of intelligence, of knowledge, of emotion. A global fiesta, intelligent and amorous, that would cover the entire surface of the earth. To create this fiesta, he struggles constantly and offers all he has: his genius, his imagination, his words and his actions. He struggles, at every moment, to eliminate fear and stupidity in man. Because of his profound desire to help to transform the society in which he lives into a more beautiful, healthier, less painful and more intelligent one, and because he puts at the service of this ineluctable and positive Social Revolution all of his creative strength, his constructive genius, his penetrating sensibility and his ceaseless work, Diego is continually attacked. During these last twenty years

I have seen him struggle against the complicated machinery of negative forces contrary to his push for freedom and transformation. He lives in a hostile world because the enemy is in the majority, but this does not daunt him, and for as long as he lives, new living energies of combat, courageous and profound, will emerge from his hands, his lips and his whole being.

All those who have brought a light to earth have struggled as Diego has; like them, he has no 'friends', but only allies. Those who emerge from themselves are magnificent; their brilliant intelligence, their profound and lucid knowledge of the human material within which they work, their solid experience, their wide culture, not gained from books, but inductive and deductive; their genius and their desire to construct, on the foundations of reality, a world cleansed of cowardice and lies. In the society in which he lives, all those of us are all allies who, like him, realise the imperative need to destroy the false bases of the present world.

Against the cowardly attacks directed at him Diego always reacts with firmness and a great sense of humour. He never compromises nor yields: he openly faces his enemies, most of them concealed, some courageous, counting always on reality, and never on 'illusory' or 'ideal' elements. This refusal to compromise and this rebelliousness are fundamental in Diego; they complement his portrait.

Among the many things said about Diego, these are the most common: they call him a chronic liar, a publicity-seeker and, most ridiculous of all, a millionaire. His alleged lying is in direct relation to his powerful imagination, that is, he lies as much as poets do, or children who have not yet been 'idiotised' by school or by their mothers. I have heard him tell all kinds of lies: from the most innocent ones, to the most complicated tales of characters that his imagination combines in fantastical situations and behaviour, always with a great sense of humour and a marvellous critical sense; but I have never heard him tell a stupid or banal lie. By lying, or playing at lying, he unmasks many people, he learns the interior workings of others who are much more candidly untruthful than he is, and the most curious thing about Diego's alleged lies is that, sooner or later, those involved in the imaginary combinations get angry, not because of the lie, but rather because of the truth contained in the lie, which always rises to the surface. That is when the 'henhouse goes into an uproar', for they see themselves exposed on the very terrain where they thought themselves protected. What really happens is that Diego is one of the few who dare to attack at its foundation, directly and without fear, the structure called the MORALITY of the hypocritical society in which we live, and since the truth doesn't sin but makes people uncomfortable, those who are exposed in their most hidden secret motives can only call Diego a liar, or, at least, an exaggerator.

They say he seeks publicity. I have noticed rather that others try to do so through him, for their own interests, only they do it with misapplied Jesuitical methods, because generally it 'backfires' on them. Diego doesn't need publicity and still less the kind offered him in his own country. His work speaks for itself. Not only for what he has done in the land of Mexico, where he is shamelessly insulted more than anywhere else, but also in every civilised country in the world, where he is recognised as one of the most important men and greatest geniuses in the cultural field. It is incredible, to be sure, that the meanest, most cowardly and stupidest insults against Diego have been vomited out in his own home: Mexico. Through the press, by means of acts of barbarism and vandalism aimed at destroying his work, using everything from the innocent parasols of 'decent' ladies who hypocritically scratch his paintings, just in passing, to acids and kitchen knives, not to forget simple, everyday spitting, worthy of those who have as much saliva as they lack brains; by means of signs on street corners bearing words little suited to such a Catholic people; by means of groups of 'well-bred' young people who throw stones at his house and his studio, destroying irreplaceable works of pre-Hispanic Mexican art – which form part of Diego's collections – and who run off after 'playing their tricks'; by means of anonymous letters (useless to speak of the worth of those who send them) or by means of the neutral, Pilatian silence of the powerful, in charge of caring for and imparting culture for the sake of the good name of the country, who give 'no importance' to these attacks against the work of a man who, with all of his genius, his creative efforts, alone, tries to defend, not only for himself, but for all, freedom of expression. All of these manoeuvres in the shadows and in the light are carried out in the name of democracy, of morality and of 'Long Live Mexico! – Long Live Christ the King!', [which] is also used at times.

All this publicity that Diego neither seeks nor needs proves two things: that the work, the entire oeuvre, the unquestionable personality of Diego are of such importance that they have to be taken into account by those whose hypocrisy and shameless arriviste plans he denounces; and the weak and deplorable state of a country – a semi-colonial one – that allows things to happen in 1949 that could only take place in the Middle Ages, at the time of the Holy Inquisition or while Hitler ruled in the world.

In order to grant recognition to the man, to the marvellous painter, to the brave fighter and upright revolutionary, they await his death. For as long as he lives, there will be plenty of 'machos', the kind schooled in the libel, who will continue to throw stones at his house, insult him anonymously or in the press of his own country and others, still more 'macho', who say nothing, but will wash their hands of it all and go down in history wrapped in the flag of prudence.

And they call him a millionaire … The only truth in this matter of Diego's millions is this: that since he is an artisan, and not a proletarian, he possesses his tools of production – that is, of his work – a house to live in, some rags to throw on and a ramshackle truck that he makes use of as a tailor his scissors. His treasure is a collection of marvellous works of sculpture, jewels of indigenous art, the living heart of true Mexico, which with indescribable economic sacrifices he has succeeded in collecting over more than thirty years to place in a museum that he has been building for the last seven. He has erected this work by his own creative effort and his own economic effort, that is, with his marvellous talent and with what he is paid for his paintings; he will donate it to the country, bequeathing to Mexico the most prodigious source of beauty that has ever existed, a gift for the eyes of those Mexicans that have them and an incalculable admiration for those from other places. Except for this, he has nothing economically; he has nothing but the strength of his work. Last year he didn't have enough money to be released from the hospital, after suffering a bout of pneumonia. Still convalescent, he started to paint to cover daily expenses and the wages of the workers who, as in the Renaissance guilds, collaborate with him in constructing the marvellous work in the Pedregal.

But insults and attacks do not change Diego. They form part of the social phenomena of a world in decadence and nothing else. All of life continues to interest and astonish him, because it changes, and everything surprises him by its beauty, but nothing disappoints him or daunts him because he understands the dialectic mechanism of phenomena and facts.

A keen observer, he has accumulated an experience that, together with his knowledge – I might almost say, his internal knowledge of things – and his intense culture, allows him to disentangle causes. Like a surgeon, he opens in order to observe, to discover what is deep and hidden and to achieve something certain, positive, that improves the circumstances and functioning of organisms. That is why Diego is neither defeatist nor sad. He is fundamentally a constructor, and above all an architect. He is an architect in his painting, in his thinking processes and in his passionate desire to structure a harmonious, functional and solid society. He always composes with precise, mathematical elements. It doesn't matter whether his composition is a painting, a house or an argument. The foundations are always reality. The poetry his works contain is that of numbers, that of the living sources of history. His laws, the solid, physical laws that govern the whole of life from atoms to suns. There is a magnificent proof of his genius as an architect in the murals that are linked, and live, with the very construction of the building that contains them, with their own organised and material function.

The stupendous work he is constructing in the village of San Pablo Tepetlapa, which he calls *el anahuacalli* (the 'house of Anahuac'), intended to house his matchless collection of ancient Mexican sculpture, is a link between ancient and new forms, a magnificent creation that will preserve and revive the incomparable architecture of the land of Mexico. It grows out of the incredibly beautiful landscape of the Pedregal like an enormous cactus looking towards the Ajusco, sober and elegant, strong and refined, ancient and perennial; it cries out, with voices of centuries and days, from its entrails of volcanic rock: Mexico is alive! Like the Coatlicue, it contains life and death; like the magnificent terrain on which it is erected, it embraces the earth with the firmness of living and permanent plant.

Always working, Diego does not live what could be called a normal life. His capacity of energy breaks clocks and calendars. Materially, he lacks time to struggle, without rest, constantly planning and executing his work. He generates and receives waves that are difficult to compare to others, and the results of his receiving and creative mechanism, being so vast and so immense, never satisfy him. Images and ideas flow through his brain at a different rhythm than usual and thus his intensity of fixation and his desire always to do more are uncontainable. This mechanism makes him indecisive. His indecisiveness is superficial because, finally, he manages to do whatever he wants with a sure and determined will. Nothing better exemplifies this modality of his character than a story his Aunt Cesarita, his mother's sister, once told me. She recalled that when Diego was a small child he went into a store, one of those sundries stores full of magic and surprises that we all remember with affection, and standing before the counter with a few centavos in his hand he surveyed the entire universe contained within the store and shouted in fury and exasperation: 'What do I want!' The store was called El Porvenir ('The Future'), and this indecision of Diego's has lasted all his life. But though he seldom makes up his mind to choose, he carries a vector line inside him that goes straight to the centre of his will and his desire.

Ever curious as he is, he is at the same time an eternal conversationalist. He can paint for hours and days without resting, chatting while he works. He discusses and talks about everything, absolutely everything, taking pleasure, like Walt Whitman, in those who want to listen to him. His conversation is always interesting. He forms phrases that astound, and that wound at times; on other occasions they move one, but they never leave the person listening with an impression of uselessness or emptiness. His words are tremendously disquieting, because they are living and true. The crudity of his ideas unnerves and disorients the listener because none of them conform to established norms of behaviour; they always cut through the bark to let the bud sprout forth; they wound to create new cells. To some people, to the strongest, Diego's conversation and truth content seem monstrous, sadistic, cruel; others, the weakest, are annulled and annihilated by it, and their defence consists of calling him a liar and a fabulist. But all try to defend themselves much as those who defend themselves against a vaccine when they receive it for the first time in their lives. They invoke hope or something that will free them from the danger of the truth. But Diego is stripped of faith, of hope, of charity. He is extraordinarily intelligent by nature and does not accept phantasms. Tenacious in his opinions, he never yields, and he defrauds all those who shield themselves behind beliefs or false goodness. That is why they call him amoral and – really – he has nothing to do with those who accept moral laws and norms.

In the midst of the storm that the clock and the calendar represent for him, he tries to do and let others do what he considers just in life: to work and to create. He considers other directions important enough to contend with, that is, he never despises the worth of others, but he defends his own, because he knows that it means rhythm and proportional relation with the world of reality. In exchange for pleasure, he gives pleasure; in exchange for effort, he exerts effort. More talented than others, he gives a much greater quantity and quality of sensibility and asks only understanding in return. Often he does not even get that, but he does not therefore submit himself or surrender. Many of the conflicts his superior personality causes in daily life come of this natural disturbance provoked by his revolutionary ideas with regard to those subject to rigidity and norms. The 'household' problems that various women have had near Diego consist of the same thing. Diego has a profound class consciousness and awareness of the role other social classes play in the general functioning of the world. Among those of us who have lived near him, some have wanted to ally themselves to the cause for which he works and struggles, and others have not. This has originated a series of conflicts in which he has been involved, but for which he is not responsible, since his position is clear and transparent. His human unity, without prejudices, whether from genius, upbringing or transformation, is not responsible for the incapacity of others, nor for the consequences this incapacity might have on social life. He works for all forces to be used and organised with greater harmony.

What weapons can be used to struggle in favour of or against a being who is closer to reality, more within the truth, if these weapons are moral, that is, conditioned by the expedience of a certain individual or human sector? Naturally they have to be amoral, not subject to what has been established or accepted as good or evil. I believe – in the fullness of my responsibility – that I cannot be against Diego, and if I am not one of his staunchest allies, I would like to be. From my position in this attempted portrait many things can be deduced, depending on who is making the deductions; but my truth, the only one I can give about Diego, is here. Limpid, not to be measured by 'sincerometres', which do not exist, but with the conviction of what concerns me, my own experience.

No words can express Diego's immense tenderness for things that possess beauty; his affection for beings without a place in the present class society; or his respect for those oppressed by it. He holds special adoration for the Indians to whom is he linked by blood; he loves them intimately for their elegance, their beauty and because they are the living flower of the cultural tradition of America. He loves children, all animals, with special predilection for Mexican hairless dogs, and birds, and plants and stones. He loves all beings, without being docile or neutral. He is very affectionate, but never surrenders himself; for this reason, and because he barely has time to dedicate himself to personal relationships, he is called ungrateful. He is respectful and refined and nothing makes him angrier than lack of respect for others and abuse. He cannot bear cheating or underhanded deception; what in Mexico is called *tomadura de pelo*. He prefers intelligent enemies to stupid allies. By temperament he is rather cheerful, but it irritates him enormously to have time taken away from his work. His recreation is work itself; he detests social gatherings and is enchanted by truly popular fiestas. At times he is timid, and just as he delights in conversing and talking with everyone, he loves to be absolutely alone at times. He is never bored because everything interests him; studying, analysing and going more deeply into all manifestations of life. He is not sentimental but he is intensely emotional and passionate. Inertia exasperates him because he is a continual current, living and potent.

Possessed of extraordinarily good taste, he admires and appreciates everything that contains beauty, whether it vibrates in a woman or a mountain. Perfectly balanced in all his emotions, his sensations and his actions, moved by materialist dialectic, precise and real, he never surrenders himself. Like the cactuses of his birthplace, he grows strong and astonishing, even on sand or stone; he blossoms with the most vivid red, the most transparent white and solar yellow; clad in thorns, he keeps his tenderness within; he lives on his strong sap amid ferocious surroundings; he illuminates in solitude like the sun that avenges the grey of the stone; his roots live in spite of being torn from the earth, surviving the anguish of solitude and sadness and all the weaknesses that subdue other beings. He rises with surprising strength and, as no other plant, blossoms and bears fruit.

Extract from Frida Kahlo, 'Portrait of Diego', *Fifty years of artistic work*, Palacio de Belles Artes, Mexico DF, 1949, as published in English in Raquel Tibol (ed), Gregory Dechant (trans), *Frida by Frida: selection of letters and texts*, Editorial RM, Mexico, 2006, pp 344–57.

DIEGO RIVERA

–

Last hour

1915

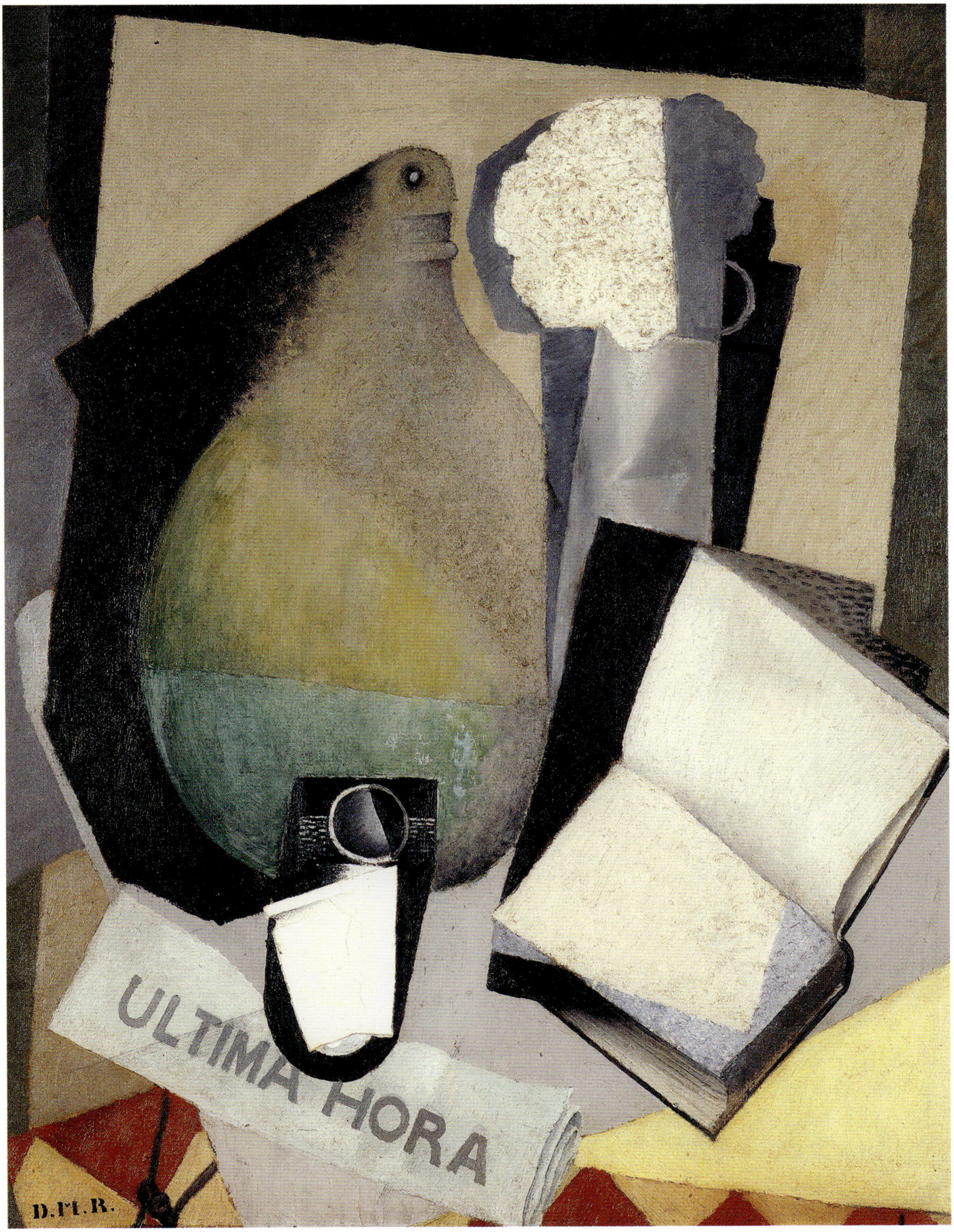
ULTIMA HORA
D.M.R.

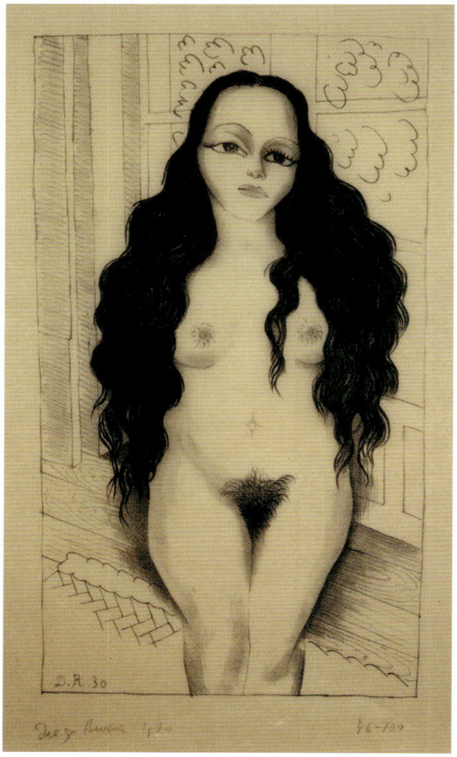

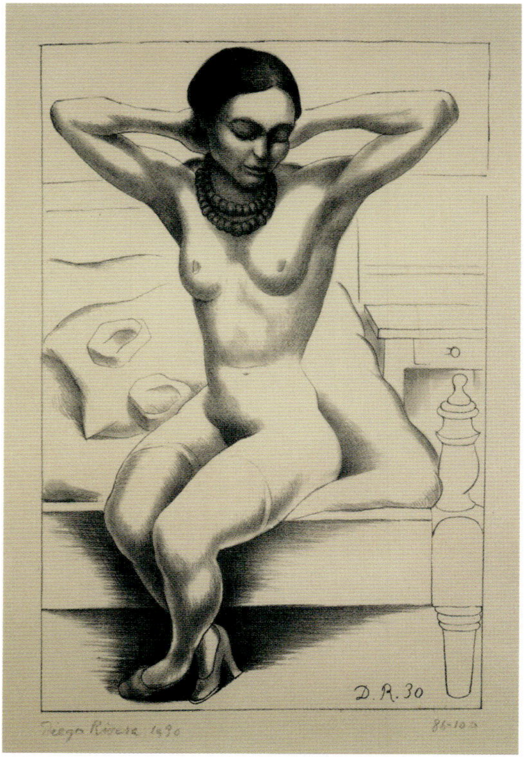

DIEGO RIVERA

–

from left

Nude with long hair (Dolores Olmedo) 1930

Nude (Frida Kahlo) 1930

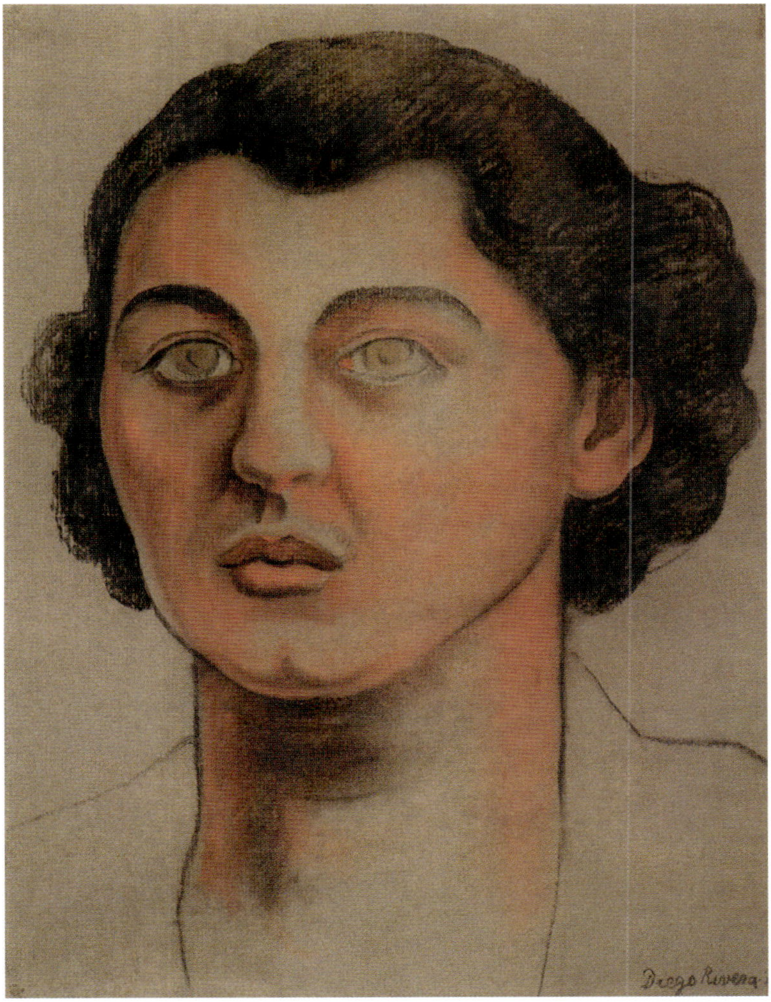

DIEGO RIVERA

–

Portrait of Cristina Kahlo

1934

DIEGO RIVERA

–

Landscape with cacti

1931

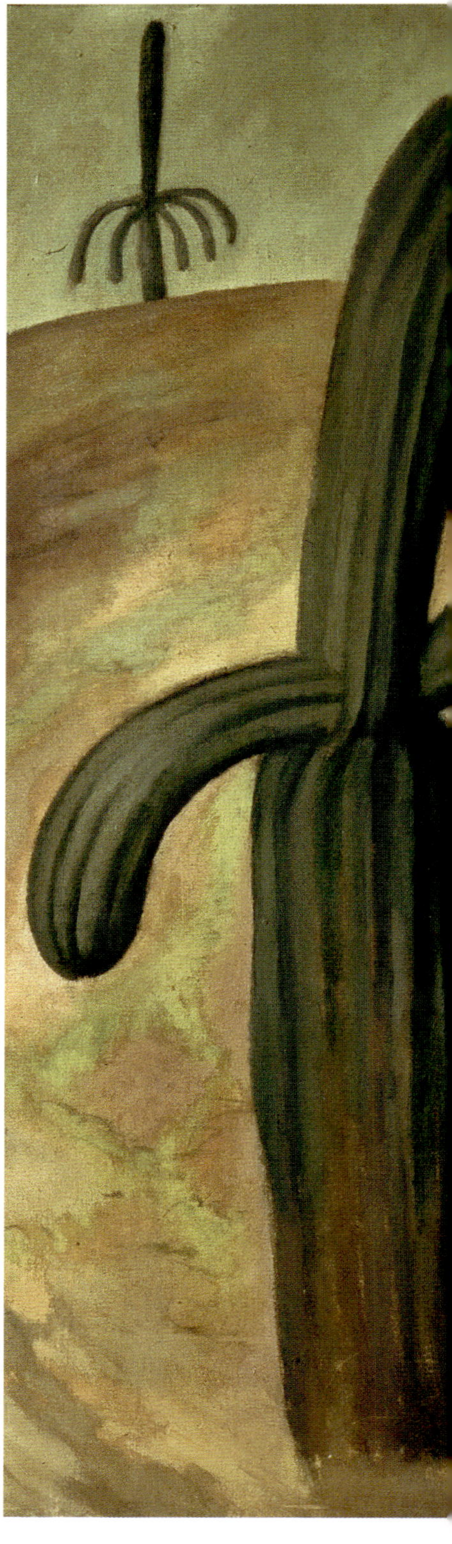

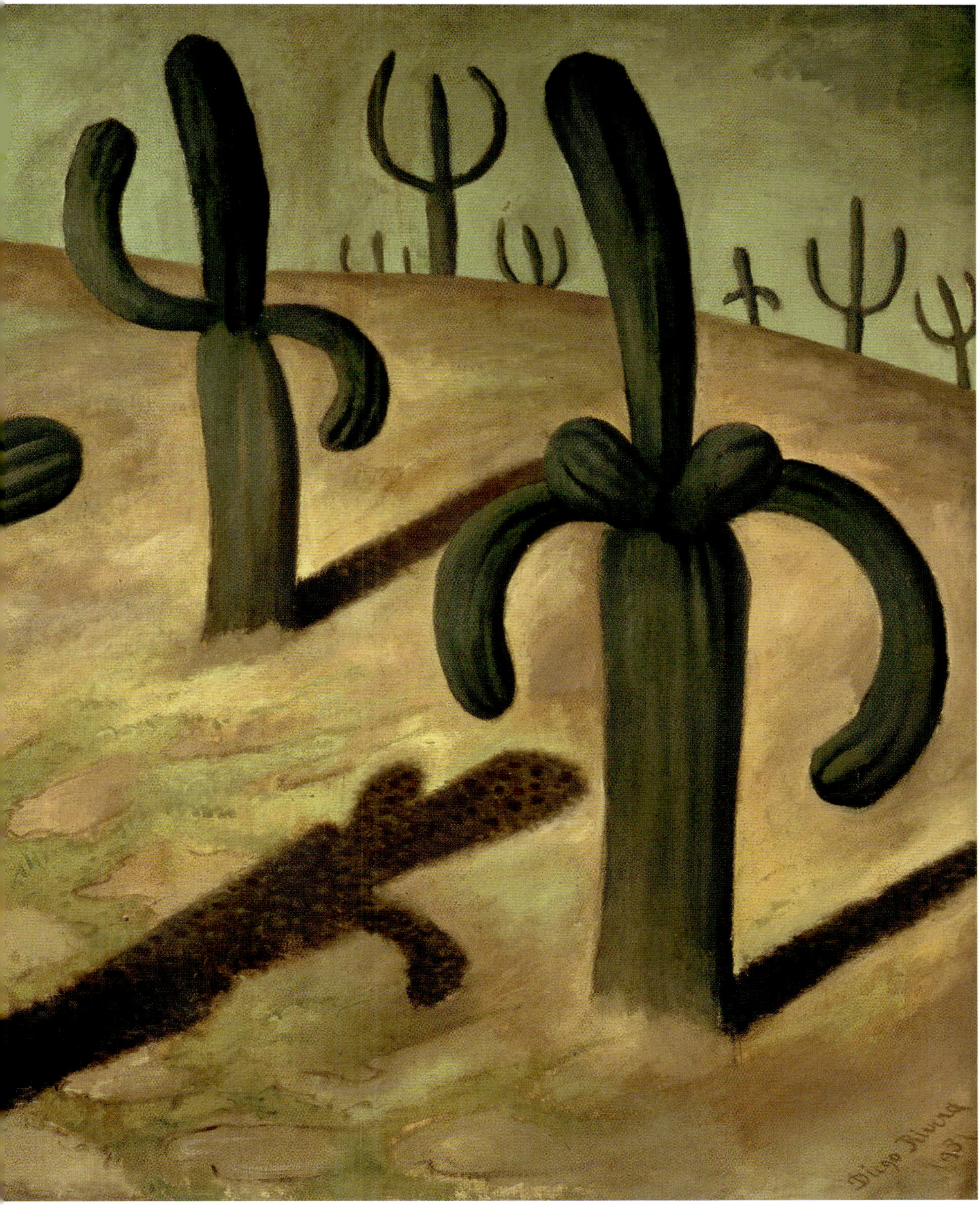
Diego Rivera
1931

DIEGO RIVERA

–

Sunflowers

1943

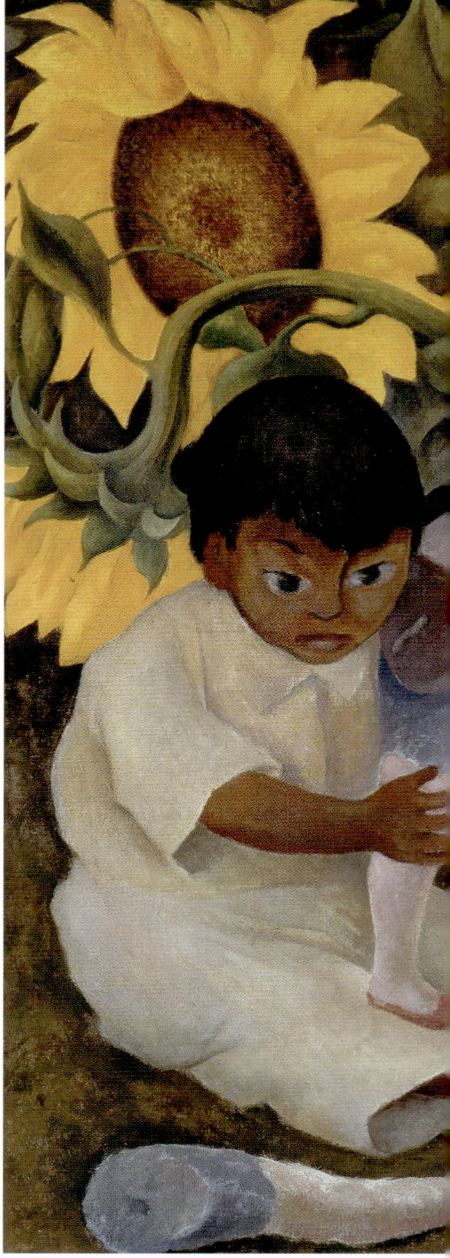

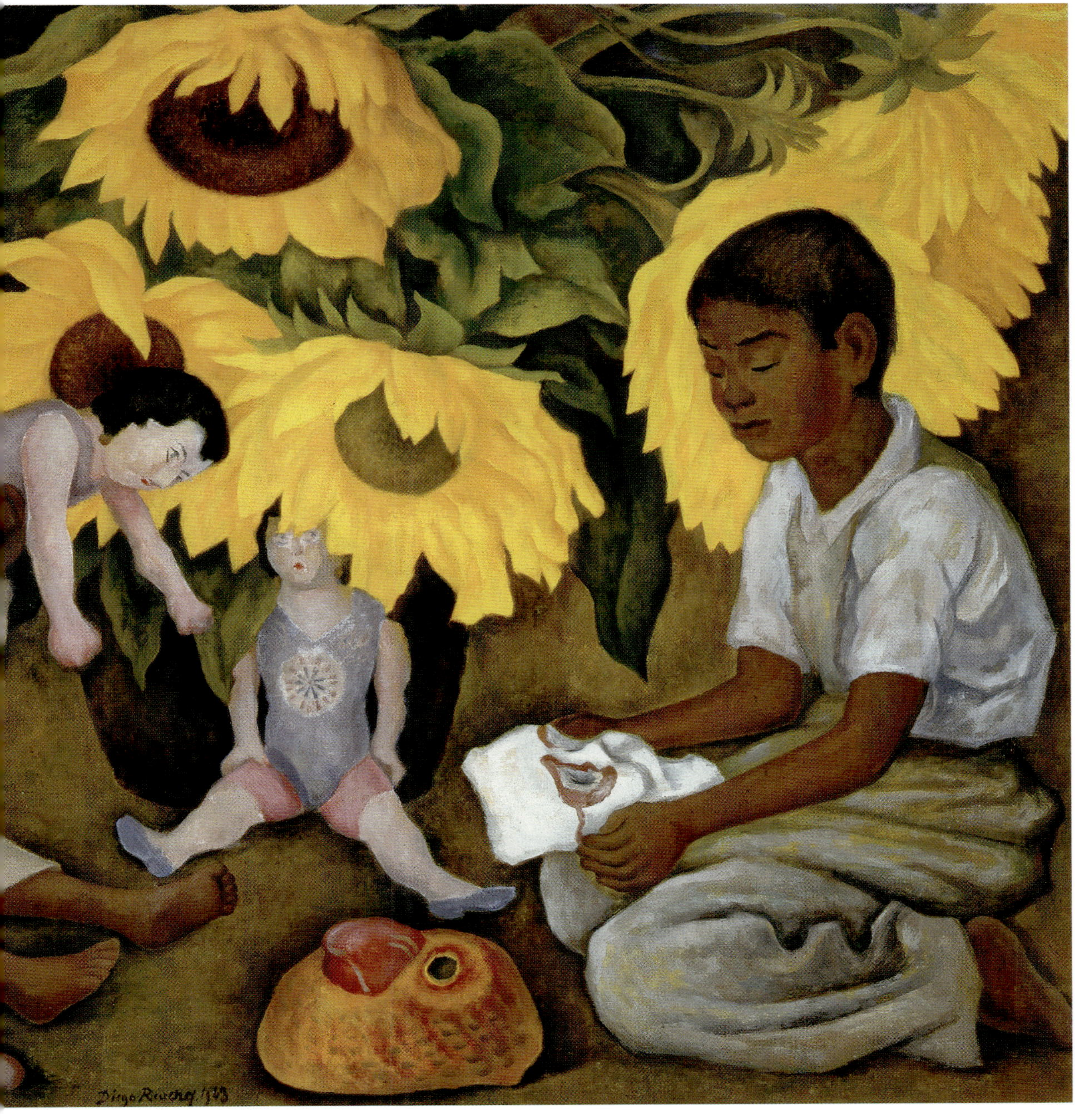
Diego Rivera 1943

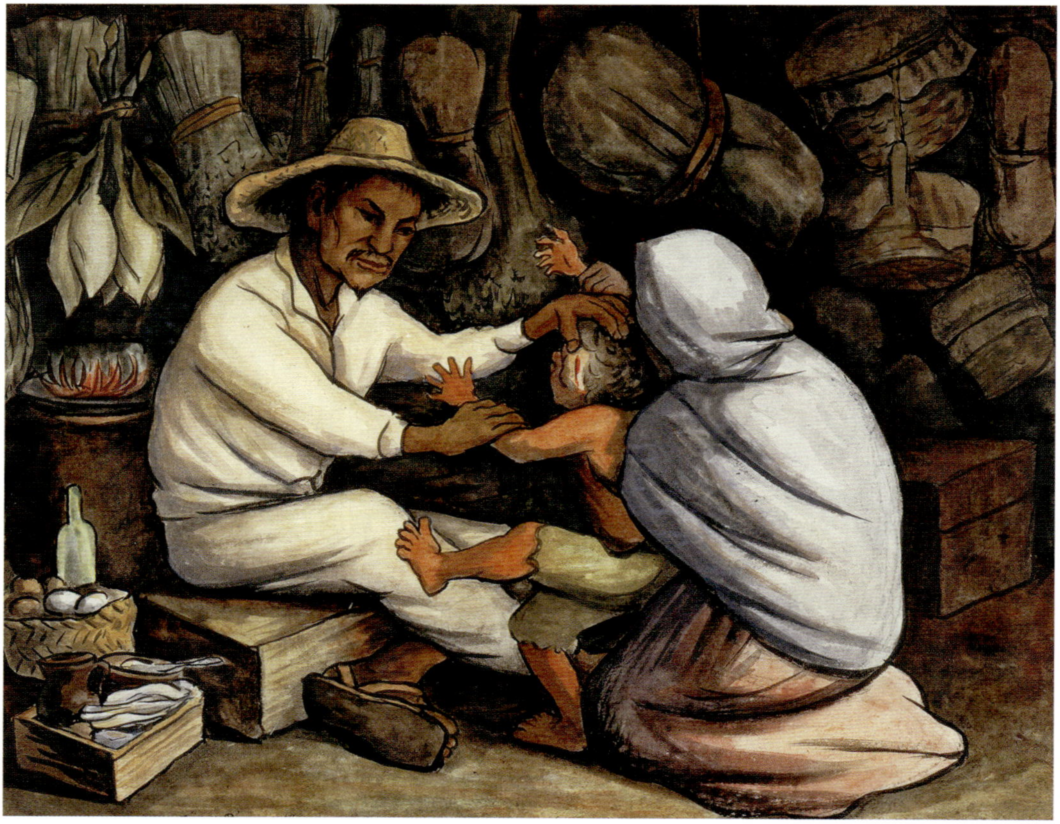

DIEGO RIVERA

—

The healer

1943

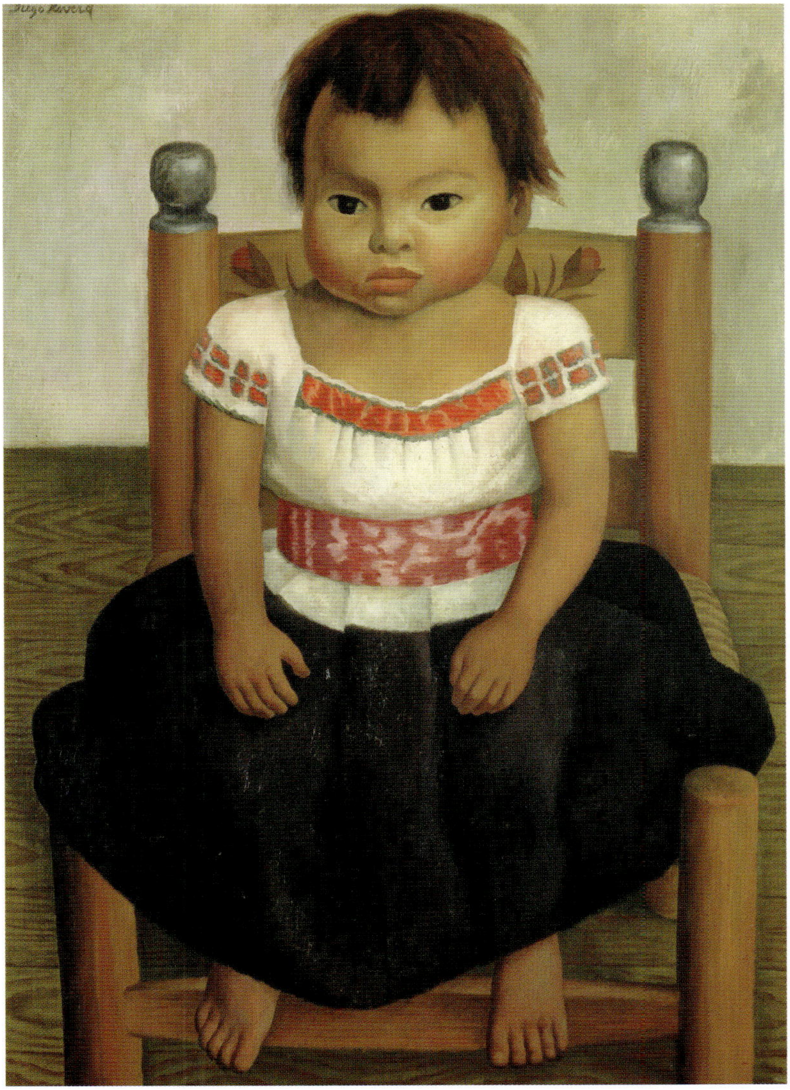

DIEGO RIVERA

–

Modesta

1937

DIEGO RIVERA

–

Calla lily vendor

1943

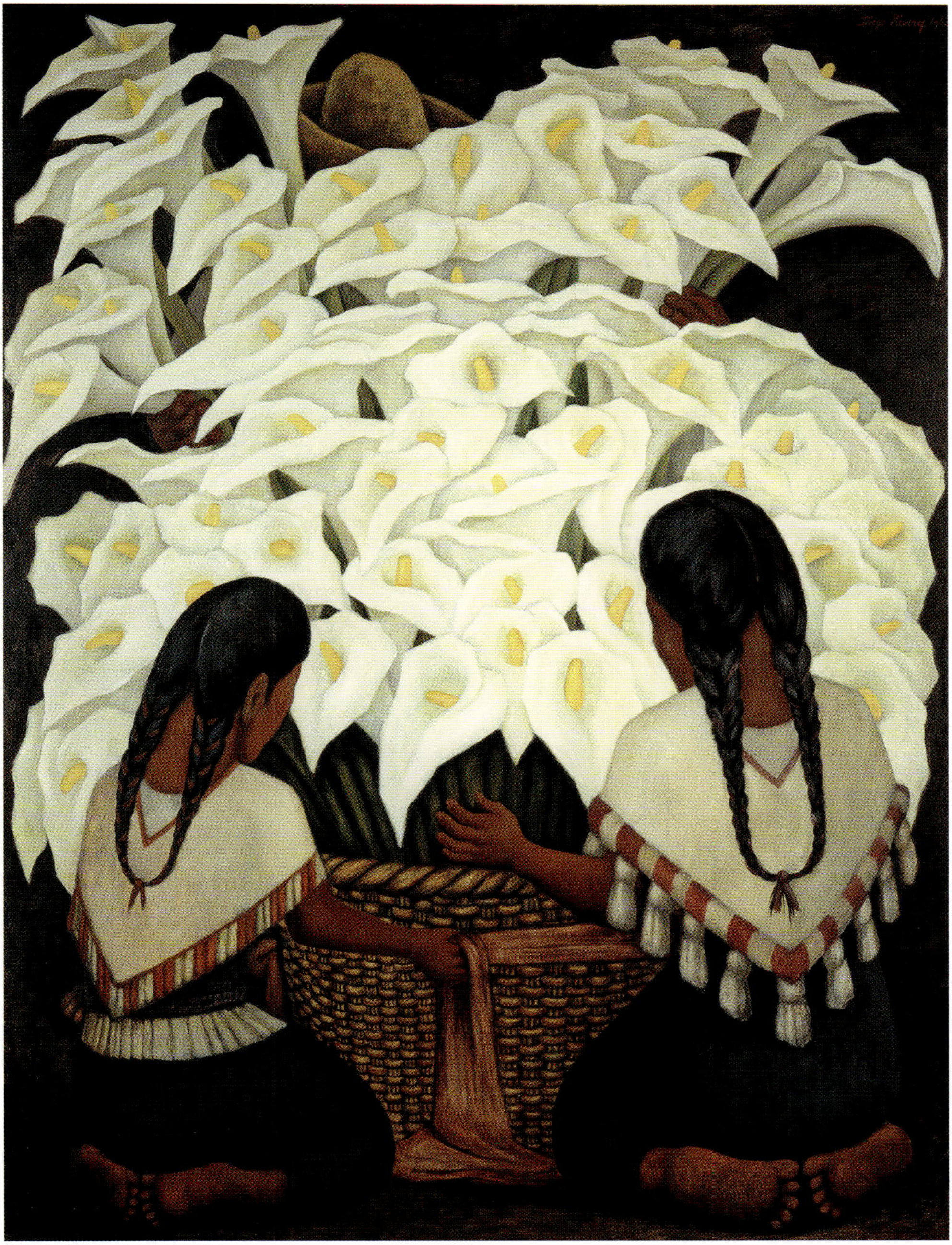

DIEGO RIVERA

–

Portrait of Natasha Gelman

1943

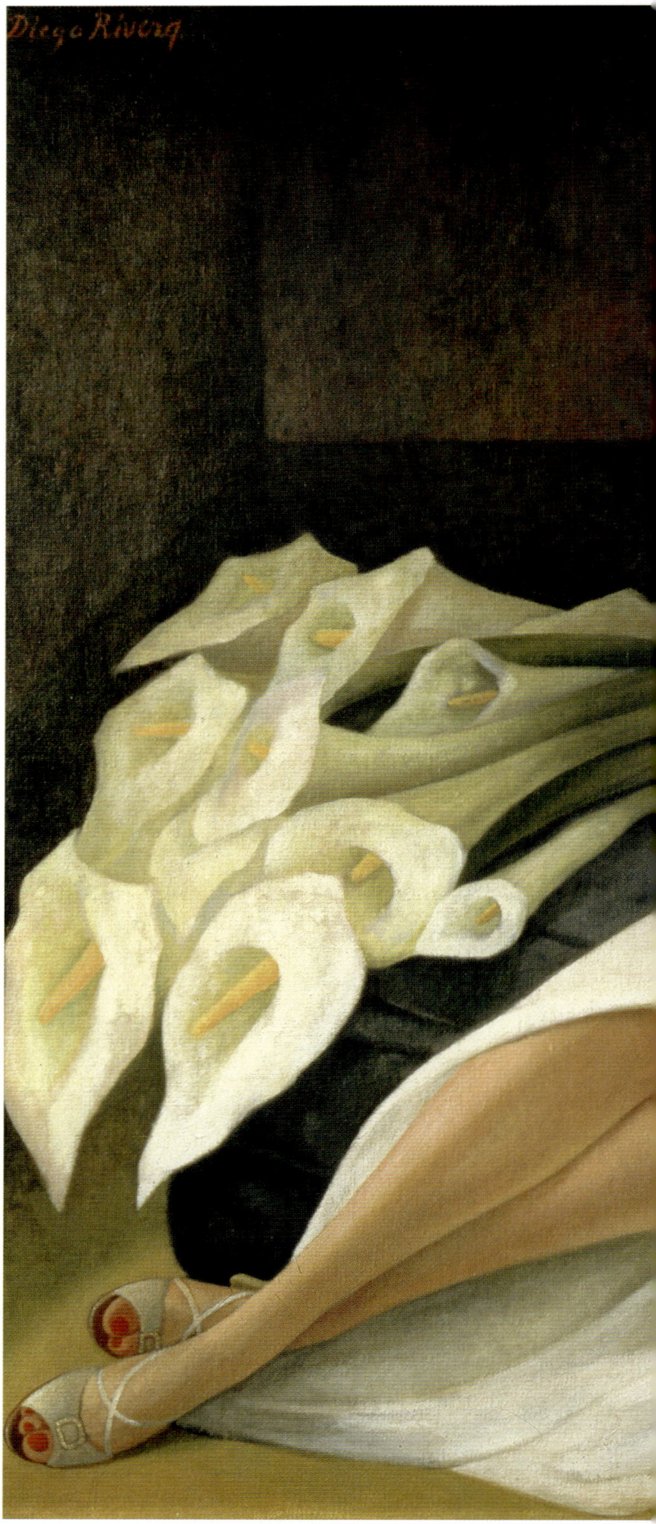

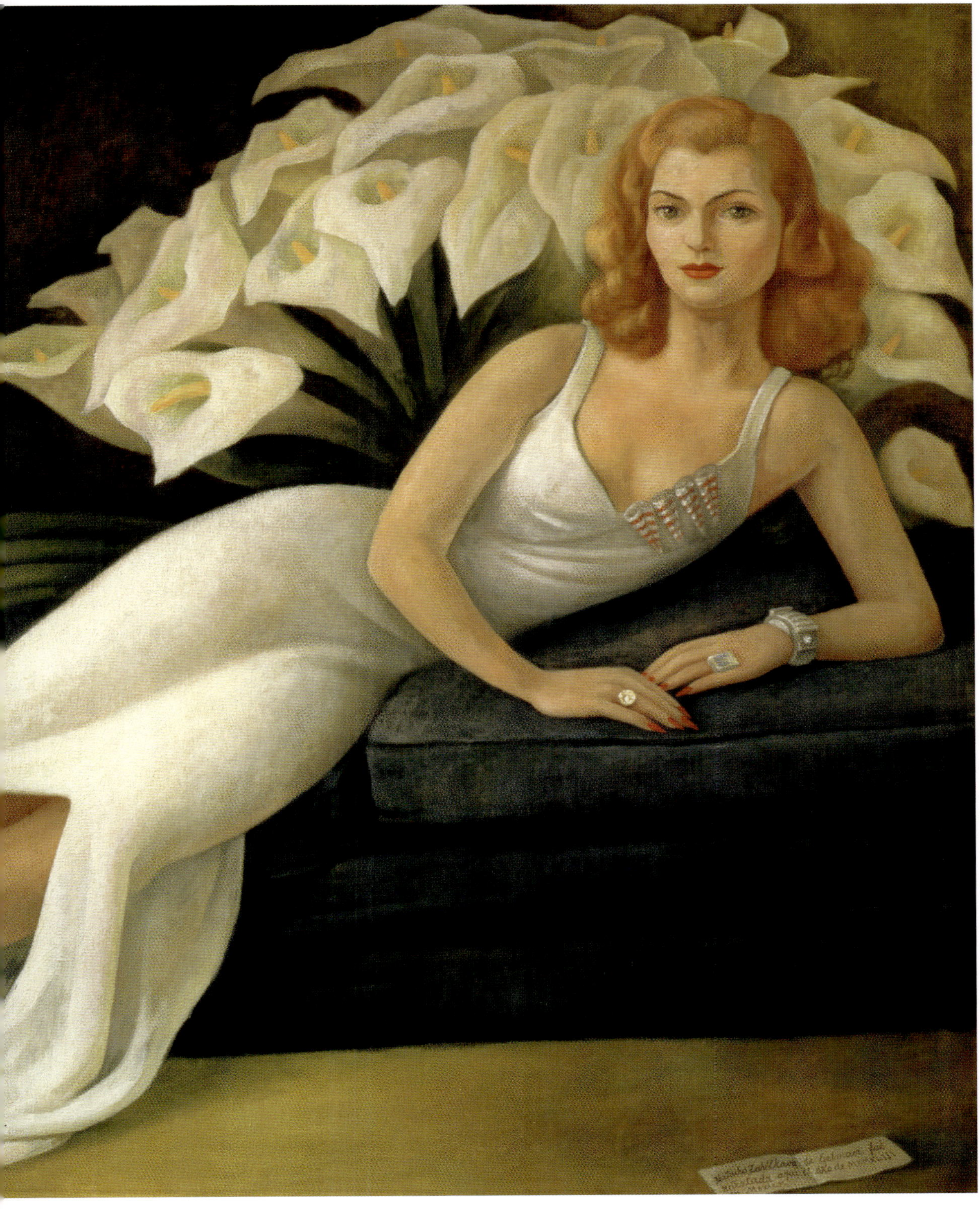

'Frida is the only example in the history of art of someone who tears open her heart and breast to tell the biological truth about what she feels in them.'

DIEGO RIVERA

–

Frida and Diego kissing following their second marriage after signing their marriage certificate, San Francisco 1940
Photographer unknown

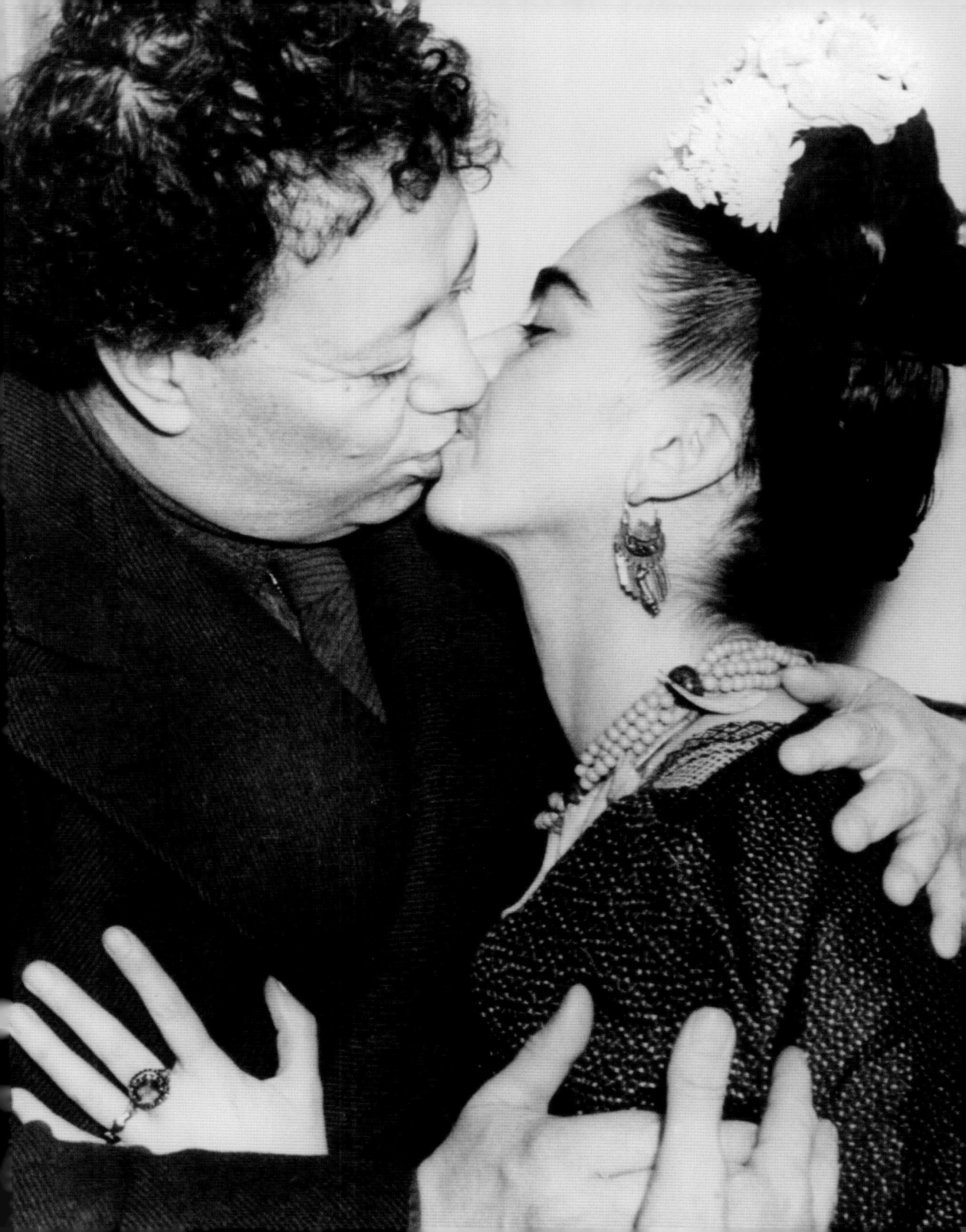

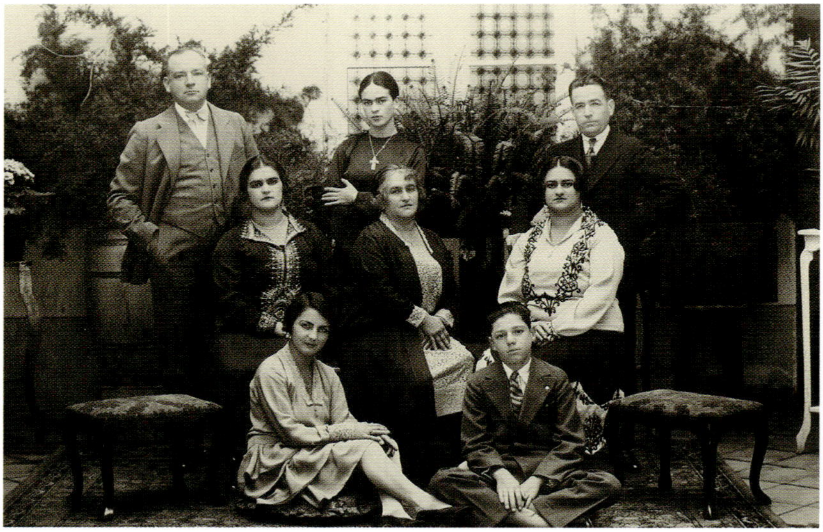

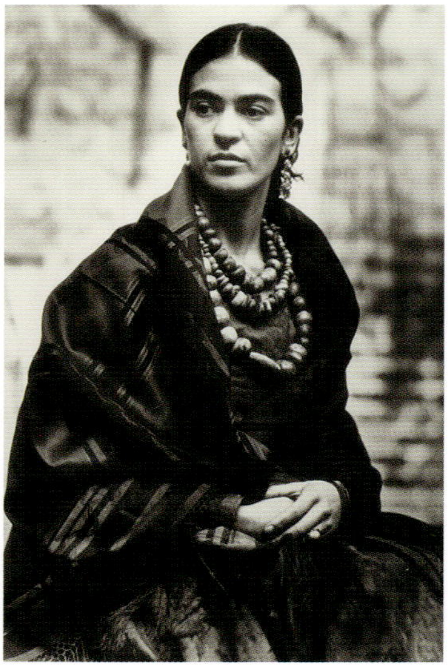

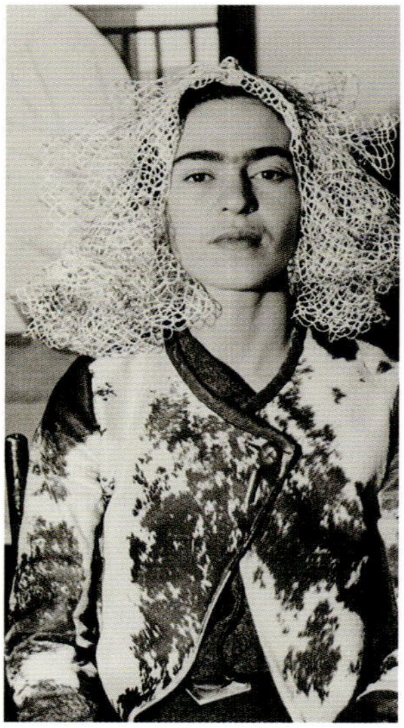

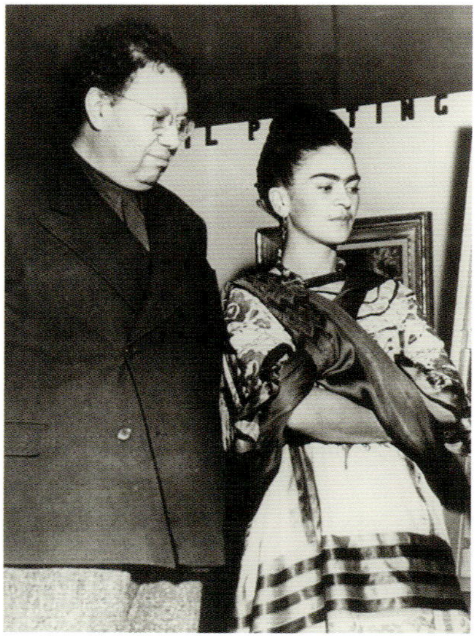

clockwise from top left:

Guillermo Kahlo
Family portrait with Frida Kahlo as young girl, 29 January 1928

Edward Weston
Frida Kahlo 1930

Lola Alvarez Bravo
Frida Kahlo 1943

Bernard Silberstein
Frida with objects on shelves c1940

Lucienne Bloch
Frida with doily on her head 1935

Untitled (Diego and Frida) c1930
Photographer unknown

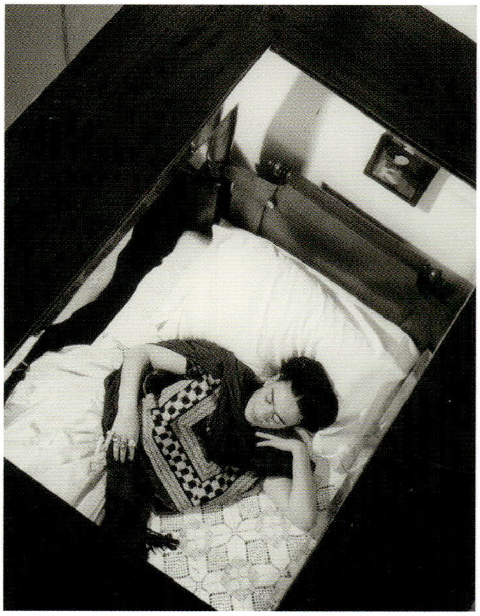

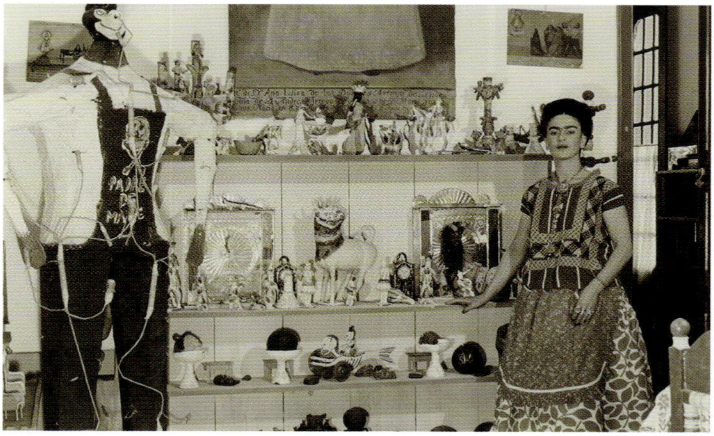

Frida and Diego: a timeline

1886

8 December: José Diego María Rivera y Barrientos is born.

1906

Rivera graduates from the Academy of San Carlos. He gains a scholarship for European travel and study.

1907

Rivera begins fourteen-year stay in Europe.

6 July: Magdalena Carmen Frieda Kahlo y Calderón is born.

1910

The Mexican Revolution begins.

1911

Cubism causes a scandal at the Salon des Indépendants, Paris.

1913

Kahlo contracts polio and suffers permanent damage to her right leg and foot.

1914

In Paris, Rivera meets many artists including Pablo Picasso.

While he is visiting Mallorca, World War I begins. He remains there for many months before returning to Paris.

1916

Rivera has his first United States exhibition in New York.

1917

Political Constitution of the United Mexican States is ratified.

Russian Bolshevik Revolution.

1920

The armed phase of the Mexican Revolution ends.

1921

Nationalistic mural painting program is established by Mexican cultural ideologue José Vasconcelos.

1922

Rivera joins the Mexican Communist Party.

Rivera begins his first government-commissioned mural, *Creation*, in the Simón Bolivar Amphitheatre of the National Preparatory School, Mexico City.

Kahlo is admitted to the National Preparatory School, preparing to study medicine at university. There she watches Rivera at work.

1923

Rivera co-authors 'Manifesto of the Union of Technical Workers, Painters, Sculptors', calling for a monumental art for the people.

1925

Kahlo is travelling in a bus when it collides with a tram. She suffers serious injuries including a broken spine, and her womb and pelvis are pierced by a handrail.

1926

Kahlo returns to hospital for many months of treatment and rehabilitation. With an easel and mirror set-up, she begins painting from her hospital bed.

1927

Tenth anniversary of Russian Bolshevik Revolution. Rivera travels to the Soviet Union to take part in official celebrations.

1928

Kahlo joins the Mexican Communist Party.

Kahlo and Rivera are introduced by Kahlo's friend Tina Modotti, photographer and activist. Rivera depicts both Modotti and Kahlo in his Ministry of Education mural, *The arsenal*.

1929

21 August: Rivera and Kahlo are married in a small civil ceremony.

Rivera is expelled from the Communist Party for acceptance of anti-Communist commissions. Kahlo resigns from the party in protest.

1930

Rivera accepts several commissions and the couple move to the United States.

1931

Rivera has a solo exhibition at the Museum of Modern Art, New York.

1932

In Detroit, Kahlo is hospitalised with a miscarriage. She records the experience in two works, *Henry Ford Hospital* and *The miscarriage*.

1933

Rivera begins a mural at the RCA Building in New York, but work is suspended for his inclusion of a portrait of Lenin. The mural is destroyed in 1934.

1935

The couple separate when Kahlo learns of Rivera's affair with her sister Cristina, but soon reconcile.

1937

Kahlo's first public exhibition in Mexico is held at the National Autonomous University.

Rivera helps exiled Marxist leader Leon Trotsky gain asylum in Mexico. Trotsky and his wife Natalia Sedova come to live at Casa Azul, Kahlo and Rivera's home in Coyoacán. Kahlo and Trotsky have a brief affair.

1938

French surrealist leader André Breton spends several months in Mexico. Together with Trotsky and Rivera, he writes 'Manifesto for an independent revolutionary art'.

Kahlo's first solo exhibition is held in New York at the Julien Levy Gallery.

1939

Kahlo travels to Paris to show in *Mexique*, organised by Breton and Marcel Duchamp. On her return from Paris, Kahlo moves back to Casa Azul. Kahlo and Rivera divorce.

World War II begins.

1940

Trotsky is assassinated in his house in Coyoacán. Kahlo and Rivera are suspected of complicity in his death.

Rivera leaves for San Francisco and paints a mural at the Golden Gate International Exposition. Kahlo also has work in the exposition, at the Palace of Fine Arts.

Kahlo flies to San Francisco for medical treatment. After reconciling, the couple remarries on Rivera's fifty-fourth birthday.

1941

Rivera plans the Anahuacalli Museum in Coyoacán, designed to house his collection of pre-Columbian artefacts.

1942

Kahlo becomes a founding member of the Seminar of Mexican Culture, a state institution of intellectuals invited to develop and promote the culture of Mexico.

1943

Both Rivera and Kahlo begin teaching at La Esmeralda art school. Before long, poor health forces Kahlo to instruct her four key students, 'Los Fridos', at home.

1944

Kahlo begins the illustrated diary she will keep till her death.

1946

Kahlo is awarded the National Prize of Arts and Sciences from the Ministry of Education. She travels to New York for a bone-graft operation and is in an iron corset for months.

1948

Rivera completes his last great mural, *Dream of a Sunday afternoon in the Alameda Central*, for Mexico City's Hotel del Prado.

Kahlo rejoins the Mexican Communist Party. Despite several appeals, Rivera is not readmitted until 1954.

1949

The retrospective, *Diego Rivera: 50 years of his artistic work*, is staged at the Palace of Fine Arts, Mexico City.

1950

Rivera is one of four artists to represent Mexico at the 25th Venice Biennale.

Rivera is awarded the National Prize for Plastic Arts.

Kahlo has seven operations on her spine and spends nine months in hospital. She is confined to a wheelchair and requires constant medical care.

1951

Rivera completes his National Palace murals after twenty-nine years.

1953

Women are given the vote in Mexico.

Kahlo has her first solo exhibition in Mexico and attends the opening in a bed carried by four friends. The foot and lower part of Kahlo's right leg is amputated.

1954

13 July: Kahlo dies at Casa Azul at the age of forty-seven.

1955

Rivera travels to USSR at the invitation of the Moscow Academy of Fine Arts. While there he has experimental treatment for his recurrent cancer.

Rivera sets up a trust fund through Banco de Mexico to administer Anahuacalli and Casa Azul, which he has donated to the Mexican people.

1956

National celebrations take place on Rivera's seventieth birthday.

1957

24 November: Rivera dies at the age of seventy. He is buried in the Rotunda of Famous Men, Mexico City.

1958

Casa Azul officially opens as the Frida Kahlo Museum.

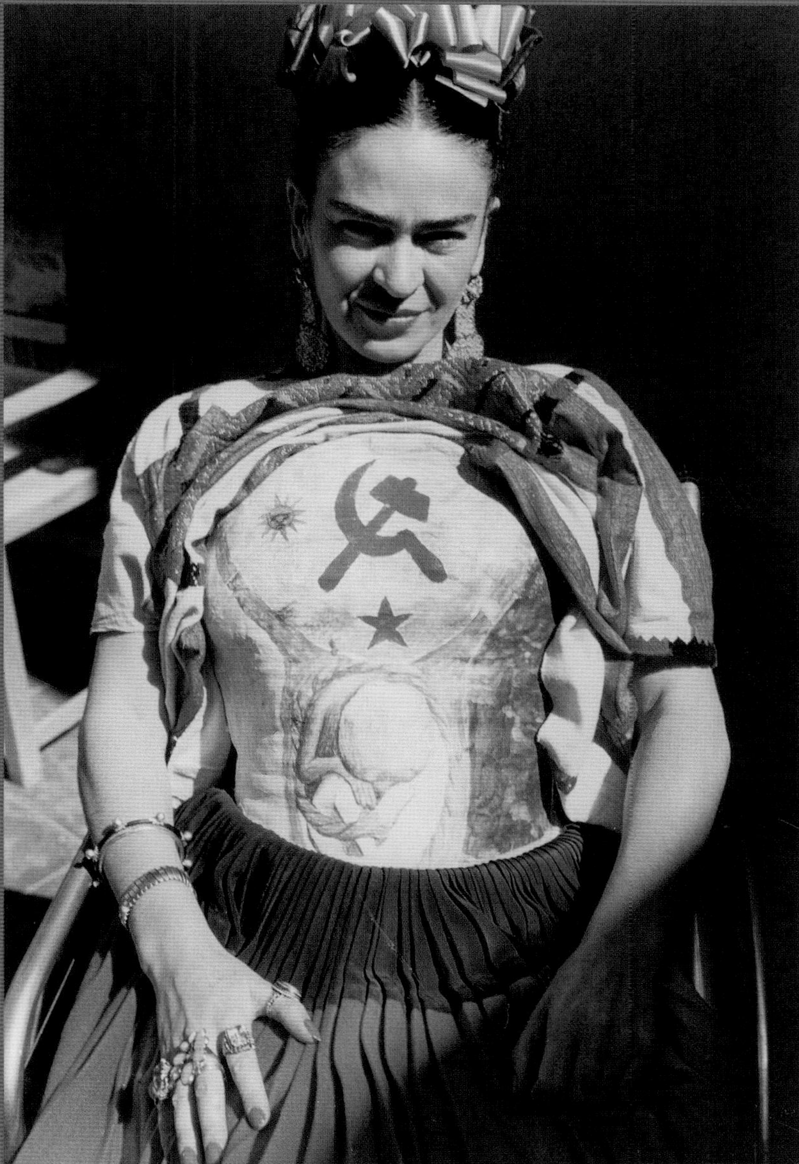

Florence Arquin
Untitled (Frida Kahlo wearing a plaster cast, which she decorated with the hammer and sickle) c1950

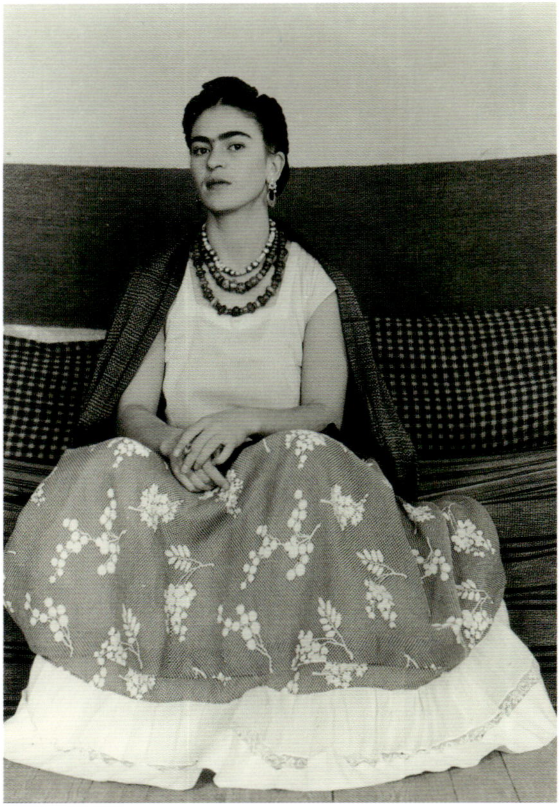
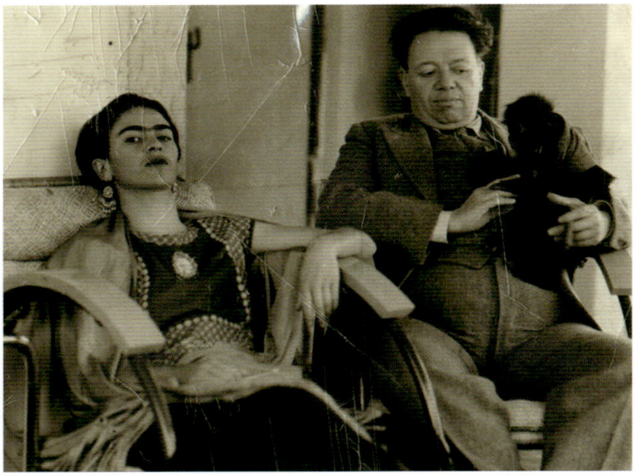
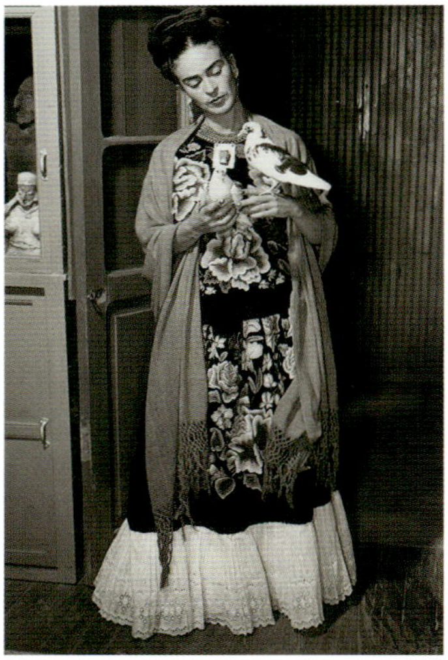

clockwise from top left:

Manuel Alvarez Bravo
Frida (seated) c1940s

Frida and Diego with Fulang Chang 1937
Photographer unknown

Juan Guzmán
Frida with two birds c1940s

Lola Alvarez Bravo
Frida Kahlo 1940s

Lola Alvarez Bravo
Frida Kahlo 1944

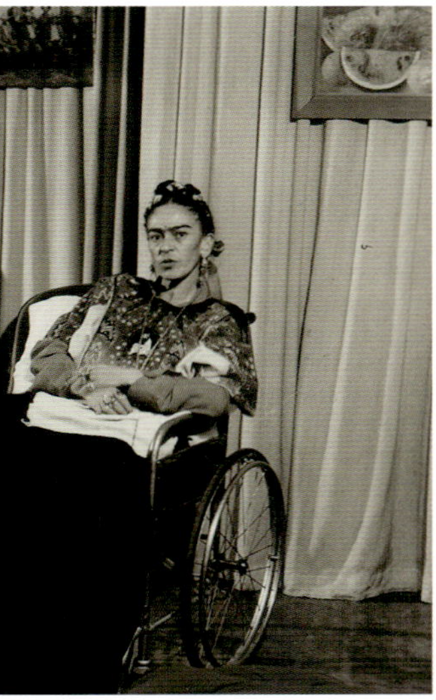
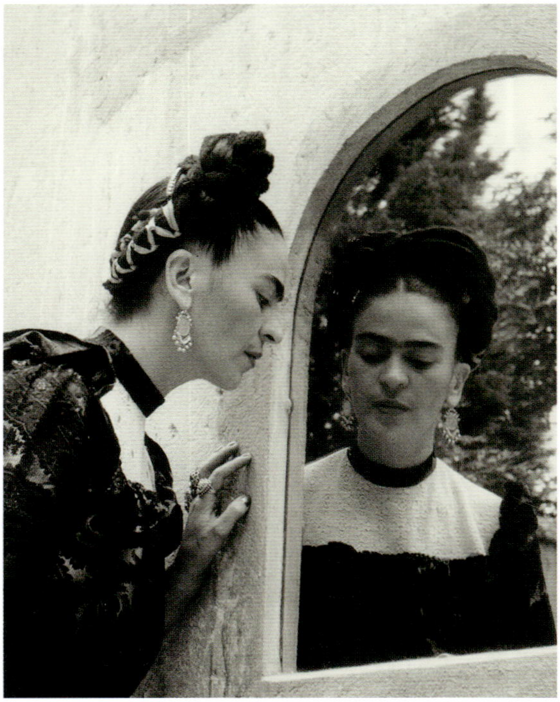

top:

Florence Arquin
Frida Kahlo, Chicago 1941

Juan Guzmán
Frida Kahlo in hospital bed holding mirror, Mexico 1950

below:

Bernice Kolko
Frida in the garden, Coyoacán 1953

Héctor García
Frida Kahlo in coffin and Diego Rivera at funeral 1954

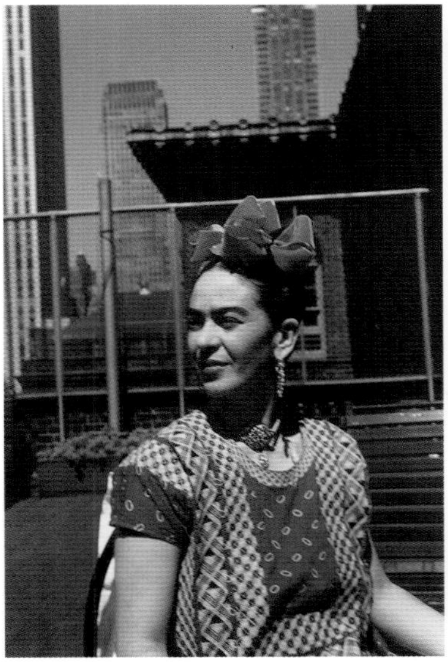

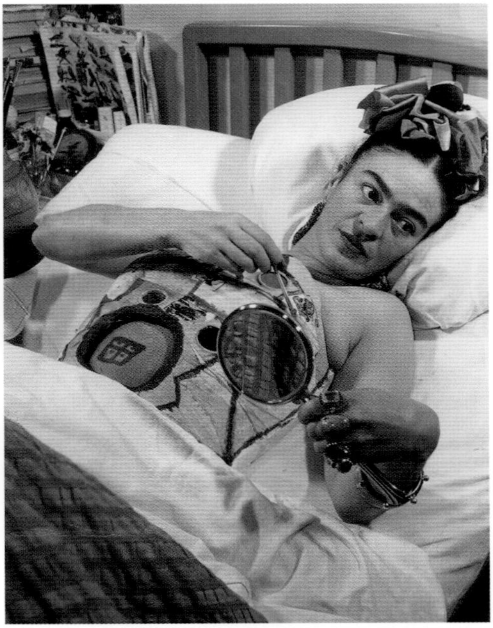

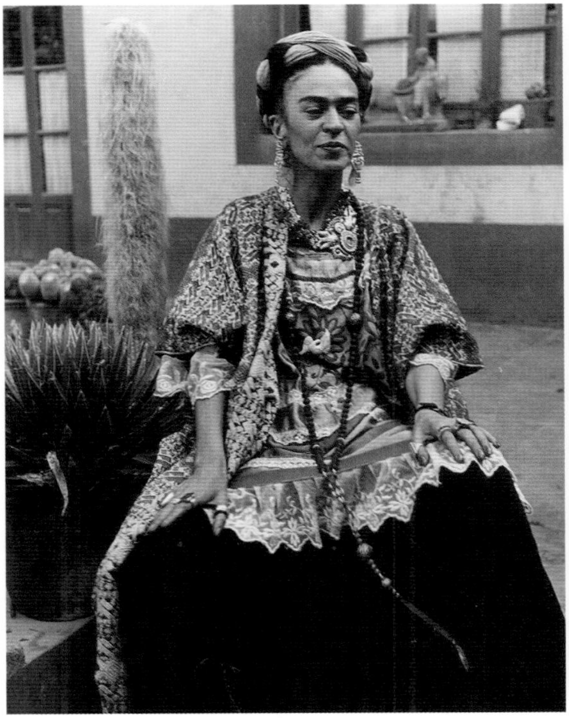

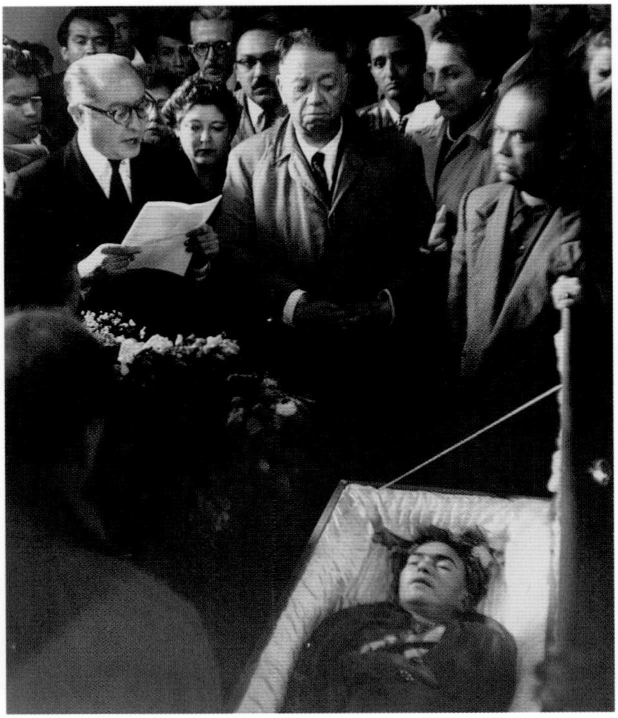

List of works

All artworks and a selection of photographs (marked •) are from the Jacques and Natasha Gelman Collection of 20th Century Mexican Art, courtesy of The Vergel Foundation and the Tarpon Trust. All other photographs are from the collection of Throckmorton Fine Art Inc.

Photographs are gelatin silver prints unless indicated otherwise.

∘ indicates work is not illustrated in the catalogue

FRIDA KAHLO
Mexico, 1907–54

The miscarriage 1932
lithographs
1st proof: 29.2 x 20.3 cm
13th proof: 31.7 x 23.5 cm

The sun peeks through the window 1932
pencil on paper
27 x 18 cm

Self-portrait with necklace 1933
oil on metal
35 x 29 cm

Portrait of Diego Rivera 1937
oil on masonite
46 x 32 cm

Self-portrait with bed (Me and my doll) 1937
oil on metal
40 x 30 cm

Self-portrait with braid 1941
oil on canvas
51 x 38.5 cm

Self-portrait with red and gold dress 1941
oil on canvas
39 x 27.5 cm

A brief 1943
coloured ink on paper
30.5 x 22.9 cm

Diego on my mind (Self-portrait as Tehuana) 1943
oil on masonite
76 x 61 cm

Portrait of Natasha Gelman 1943
oil on masonite
30 x 23 cm

Self-portrait with monkeys 1943
oil on canvas
81.5 x 63 cm

The bride who becomes frightened when she sees life opened 1943
oil on canvas
63 x 81.5 cm

Chromophore, auxochrome 1944
collage and ink
42 x 36 cm ∘

Lady Liberty (Workers of the world unite) c1945
coloured pencil on paper
28.9 x 21.6 cm

Masks (Carma I) 1946
sepia ink on paper
21.6 x 27 cm

11:25 (Carma III) 1946
sepia on paper
27.9 x 19.1 cm

Liberty c1946
sepia Conté sticks on paper
29.2 x 21.6 cm

Portrait of Arcady Boytler (recto ∘) and **Eyes** (verso) 1947
pencil and sepia ink on paper
22.3 x 21.7 cm

The love embrace of the universe, the earth (Mexico), Diego, me and and Señor Xólotl 1949
oil on masonite
70 x 60.5 cm

Untitled (Atomic bomb) c1951
charcoal on paper
29.5 x 22.2 cm

Collage with two flies c1953
collage and watercolour on cardboard
12.7 x 16.8 cm ∘

Drawing with foot nd
colour pencil and graphite on paper
21.3 x 27 cm •

DIEGO RIVERA
Mexico, 1886–1957

Last hour 1915
oil on canvas
92 x 73 cm

Nude (Frida Kahlo) 1930
lithograph, edition 86 of 101
41.3 x 27.3 cm

Nude with long hair (Dolores Olmedo) 1930
lithograph, edition 96 of 100
42 x 24.2 cm

Landscape with cacti 1931
oil on canvas
125.5 x 150 cm

Portrait of Cristina Kahlo 1934
pastel on paper
61.6 x 47.6 cm

Modesta 1937
oil on canvas
80 x 59 cm

Calla lily vendor 1943
oil on masonite
150 x 120 cm

Portrait of Natasha Gelman 1943
oil on canvas
115 x 153 cm

Sunflowers 1943
oil on canvas
90 x 130 cm

The healer 1943
gouache on paper
47 x 61 cm

PHOTOGRAPHS

Acme Photo

Diego and Frida in NYC 1933
22.9 x 17.8 cm

Florence Arquin
USA, 1900–74

Frida Kahlo, Chicago 1941
25.4 x 20.3 cm

Untitled (Frida Kahlo in Coyoacán, Mexico) early 1940s
16.5 x 25.4 cm ∘

Untitled (Frida Kahlo in wheelchair with sun umbrella) c1950
25.4 x 20.3 cm ∘

Untitled (Frida Kahlo wearing a plaster cast, which she decorated with the hammer and sickle) c1950
platinum print
11.4 x 7.6 cm

Lucienne Bloch
Switzerland/USA, 1909–99

Frida at the Barbizon Plaza Hotel 1933
29.2 x 19 cm •

New Workers School, NYC 1933
12.7 x 17.8 cm

Frida biting her necklace 1933
21.1 x 25.7 cm ∘

Frida with doily on her head 1935
25.4 x 15.2 cm

Lola Alvarez Bravo
Mexico, 1907–93

Frida Kahlo 1940s
20.3 x 25.4 cm

Frida Kahlo 1943
25.4 x 20.3 cm

Frida in front of mirrored wardrobe keeper, Casa Azul, Mexico 1945
25.4 x 20.3 cm ∘

Frida Kahlo 1944
gelatin silver print, vintage
25.4 x 20.3 cm

Arturo Estrada and Frida Kahlo in exhibition (Frida at opening, Mexico DF) c1944
20.3 x 25.4 cm ∘

Frida in bedroom 1945
25.4 x 20.3 cm ∘

Frida Kahlo's death portrait 1954
20.3 x 22.9 cm ∘

Manuel Alvarez Bravo
Mexico, 1902–2002

Frida (seated) c1940s
25.4 x 20.3 cm

Frida at the Society of Modern Art, Picasso exhibit, Mexico c1944
24.1 x 17.8 cm

Imogen Cunningham
USA, 1883–1976

Frida Kahlo 1931
33.8 x 25.4 cm

Guillermo Davila
Germany, 1872–1941

Frida 1929
49.5 x 40.6 cm

Gisele Freund
Germany/France, 1908–2000

Frida and Dr Farill 1951
31.8 x 26.2 cm ∘

Héctor García
Mexico, 1923–2012

Frida with rabbit 1940s
22.9 x 16.5 cm ∘

Frida with painting ('The love embrace') 1949
27.9 x 27.9 cm •

Frida Kahlo with Itzcuintli dog 1952
17.5 x 16.5 cm ∘

Frida Kahlo in coffin and Diego Rivera at funeral 1954
30 x 25.4 cm

Juan Guzmán
Germany/Mexico, 1911–82

Frida with two birds c1940s
platinum print
11.7 x 9.1 cm

Frida Kahlo in hospital bed holding decorated skull 1950
20.3 x 25.4 cm ∘

Frida Kahlo in hospital bed holding mirror 1950
24.1 x 19 cm

Frida and Diego by mural 'The nightmare of war and the dream of peace', the Palace of Fine Arts, Mexico 1952
gelatin silver print, vintage
24.3 x 19.1 cm

Fritz Henle
Germany/Puerto Rico, 1909–93

Frida Kahlo leaving the church in Coyoacán, Mexico 1937
25.4 x 25.4 cm ∘

Frida in front of studio with monkey, Coyoacán 1943
20.3 x 19 cm

Frida in her studio 1943
gelatin silver print, vintage
28.2 x 24.9 cm

Guillermo Kahlo
Germany/Mexico, 1871–1941

Family portrait with Frida Kahlo as young girl, 29 January 1928
20.3 x 25.4 cm

Bernice Kolko
Poland/USA, 1905–70

Untitled (Frida Kahlo with her friend Teresa Proenza) 1952
gelatin silver print, vintage
19.8 x 22.4 cm ∘

Frida in the garden, Coyoacán 1953
17.27 x 16.51 cm

Leo Matiz
Colombia, 1917–98

Untitled (Frida Kahlo on stairs looking right) c1940s
22.4 x 16 cm

The pottery shed at Talavera, Coyoacán 1946
29.2 x 29.2 cm

Martin Munkácsi
Romania/USA, 1896–1963

Diego and Frida 1934
printed later by Joan Munkácsi
35.6 x 27.9 cm •

Nickolas Muray
Hungary/USA, 1892–1965

Frida Kahlo on white bench 1938
carbon print
45.5 x 36 cm •∘

Frida Kahlo in blue dress 1939
45 x 36 cm •∘

Frida Kahlo with red 'rebozo' 1939
carbon print
45.5 x 36 cm •∘

Frida with Olmec figurine, Coyoacán 1939
colour carbon print
27.3 x 40 cm ∘

Frida Kahlo in New York 1946
46 x 33.7 cm •∘

Diego Rivera

Untitled (Frida Kahlo in her garden in Coyoacán) c1930
8.4 x 5.8 cm ∘

Emmy Lou Packard and Frida Kahlo in Coyoacán 1941
printed by Don Beatty
19 x 18.4 cm ∘

Bernard Silberstein
USA, 1905–99

Frida Kahlo in her bedroom 1940
34.3 x 27.9 cm ∘

Frida Kahlo painting 'The wounded table', Coyoacán 1940
35.3 x 43.2 cm ∘

Frida paints self-portrait while Diego observes 1940
43.2 x 35.6 cm •

Frida with flowers in her hair c1940
35.6 x 27.9 cm ∘

Frida with objects on shelves c1940
35.6 x 43.2 cm

Edward Weston
USA, 1886–1958

Frida Kahlo 1930
selenium-toned gelatin silver print
23.6 x 19.8 cm

Guillermo Zamora
Mexico, 1915–2002

Frida and Diego, Coyoacán 1937
8.4 x 5.8 cm

Photographer unknown

Untitled (Diego and Frida) c1930
24.1 x 19.8 cm

Diego observing Frida paint 'Self-portrait on the borderline', Detroit 1932
21.59 x 16.76 cm

Frida and Diego during a Mexican Labor anti-fascist demonstration in Mexico City 1936
gelatin silver print, vintage
25.4 x 20.3 cm

Frida and Diego with Fulang Chang 1937
10.2 x 12.7 cm

Frida and Diego kissing following their second marriage after signing their marriage certificate, San Francisco 1940
23.6 x 18.5 cm

Contributors

Nicholas Chambers is senior curator, modern and contemporary international art, at the Art Gallery of New South Wales. Chambers has previously worked as Milton Fine Curator of Art at the Andy Warhol Museum in Pittsburgh, USA, as well as an adjunct professor at the Department of History of Art and Architecture, University of Pittsburgh. Prior to that, he worked at the Queensland Art Gallery | Gallery of Modern Art as curator of international art.

Robert R Littman was a friend and adviser to Jacques and Natasha Gelman during their lifetimes. Littman is president and director of The Vergel Foundation, which owns and manages the Gelman Collection. He was previously director of Mexico City's Museo Rufino Tamayo and then of the Centro Cultural/Arte Contemporáneo, the contemporary art museum of the Televisa media company, also in the capital. He also serves on the board of the Fundación Cultural Parque Morelos, which oversees the Muros precinct in Cuernavaca where the Gelman Collection was on permanent view.

Published by
Art Gallery of New South Wales
Art Gallery Road, The Domain
Sydney 2000, Australia
artgallery.nsw.gov.au

in association with the exhibition

Frida Kahlo and Diego Rivera: from the Jacques and Natasha Gelman Collection

Art Gallery of New South Wales
25 June – 9 October 2016

The Heard Museum,
Phoenix, Arizona
9 April – 20 August 2017

Organised by

The Vergel Foundation and

artémios

Supported by

The Ministry of Culture
and the National Institute of
Fine Arts of Mexico

CULTURA SECRETARÍA DE CULTURA | INBA

ART GALLERY NSW PRESIDENT'S COUNCIL

The Art Gallery of New South Wales is a statutory body of the NSW State Government

Managing editor Julie Donaldson
Text editor Lisa Girault
Rights & permissions
Polly Gillman

Design Analiese Cairis
Production Cara Hickman
Prepress Spitting Image, Sydney
Printing Printed in China by
Australian Book Connection

National Library of Australia
Cataloguing-in-publication entry

Chambers, Nicholas, author, editor.
Frida Kahlo and Diego Rivera: from the Jacques and Natasha Gelman collection / Nicholas Chambers, Robert R Littman, Michael Brand (foreword).

ISBN 9781741741230
(paperback)

Subjects: Kahlo, Frida, 1907 –1954. Rivera, Diego, 1886–1957. Kahlo, Frida, 1907–1954 –Exhibitions. Rivera, Diego, 1886–1957–Exhibitions. Gelman, Jacques–Art collections –Exhibitions. Gelman, Natasha –Art collections–Exhibitions. Painting, Mexican–20th century.

759.972

Distribution

Australian and New Zealand
Thames & Hudson Australia
11 Central Boulevard, Portside
Business Park, Fishermans
Bend, Melbourne 3207
T: 03 9646 7788
E: enquiries@thaust.com.au

North America
University of Washington Press
E: washington.edu/uwpress

All other territories
Thames & Hudson UK
181A High Holborn, London
WC1V7QX
T: 44 20 7845 5000
E: sales@thameshudson.co.uk
www.thameshudson.co.uk

Photo credits

pp 8, 16: Fritz Henle © Fritz Henle Estate
pp 15, 80: Lucienne Bloch © Estate of Lucienne Bloch, courtesy Old Sage Studios
p 80: Edward Weston © Center for Creative Photography, Arizona Board of Regents
pp 80, 84: Lola Alvarez Bravo © 1995 Center for Creative Photography, the University of Arizona Foundation

Image details

front cover: Frida Kahlo *Self-portrait with necklace* 1933
back cover: Nickolas Muray *Frida and Diego with hat* 1941 © Nickolas Muray Photo Archives
p 2: Frida Kahlo *Eyes*, verso of *Portrait of Arcady Boytler* 1947
p 3: Frida Kahlo *Diego on my mind (Self-portrait as Tehuana)* 1943
p 4: Martin Munkacsi *Diego and Frida* 1934 © The Estate of Martin Munkácsi, courtesy Howard Greenberg Gallery, NY
p 91: Frida Kahlo *The love embrace of the universe, the Earth (Mexico), Diego, me and Señor Xólotl* 1949
p 92: Leo Matiz *The pottery shed at Talavera, Coyoacán* 1946

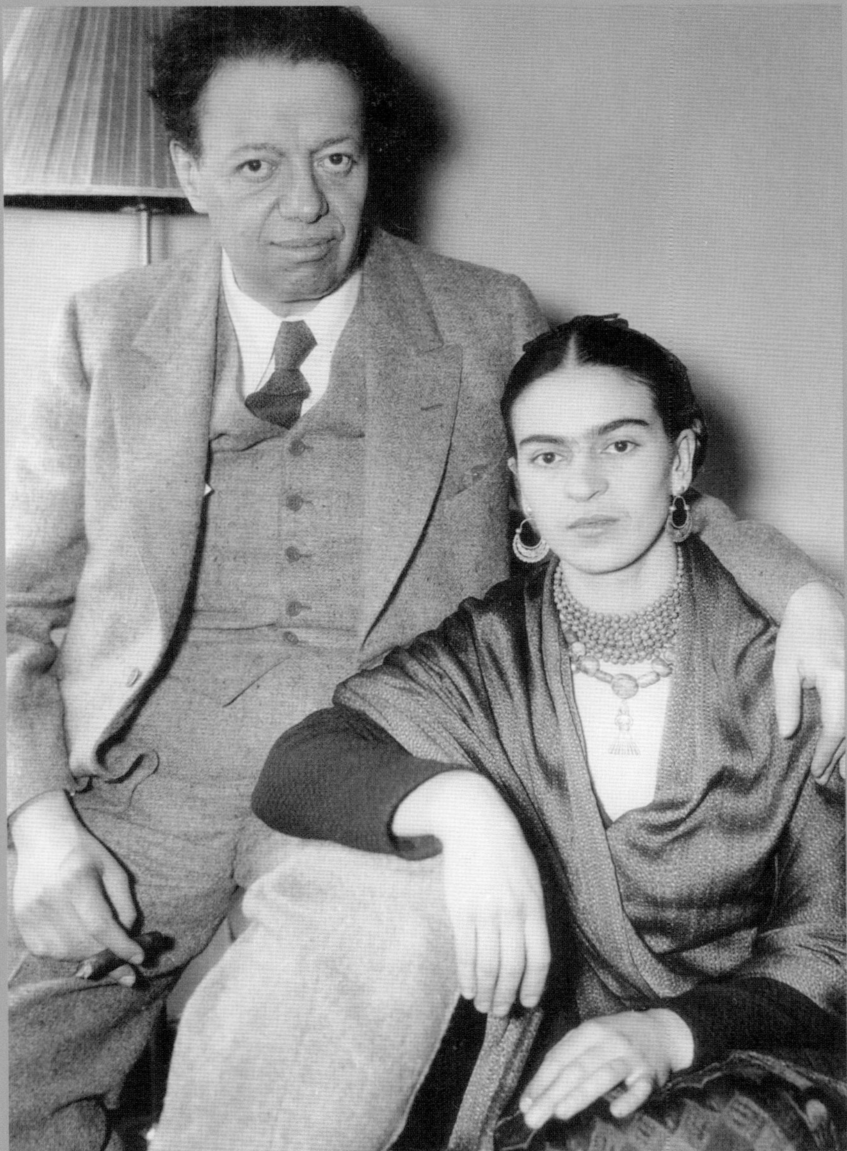

–

Diego and Frida in NYC 1933
Acme Photo

'Diego's form is that of an affectionate
monster, which the grandmother,
the Ancient Concealer, the necessary
and eternal matter, the mother
of men, and all the gods invented
by them in their delirium, out of fear
and hunger, THE WOMAN,
and among all of them – I MYSELF –
would like always to hold in her arms
like a newborn child.'

FRIDA KAHLO

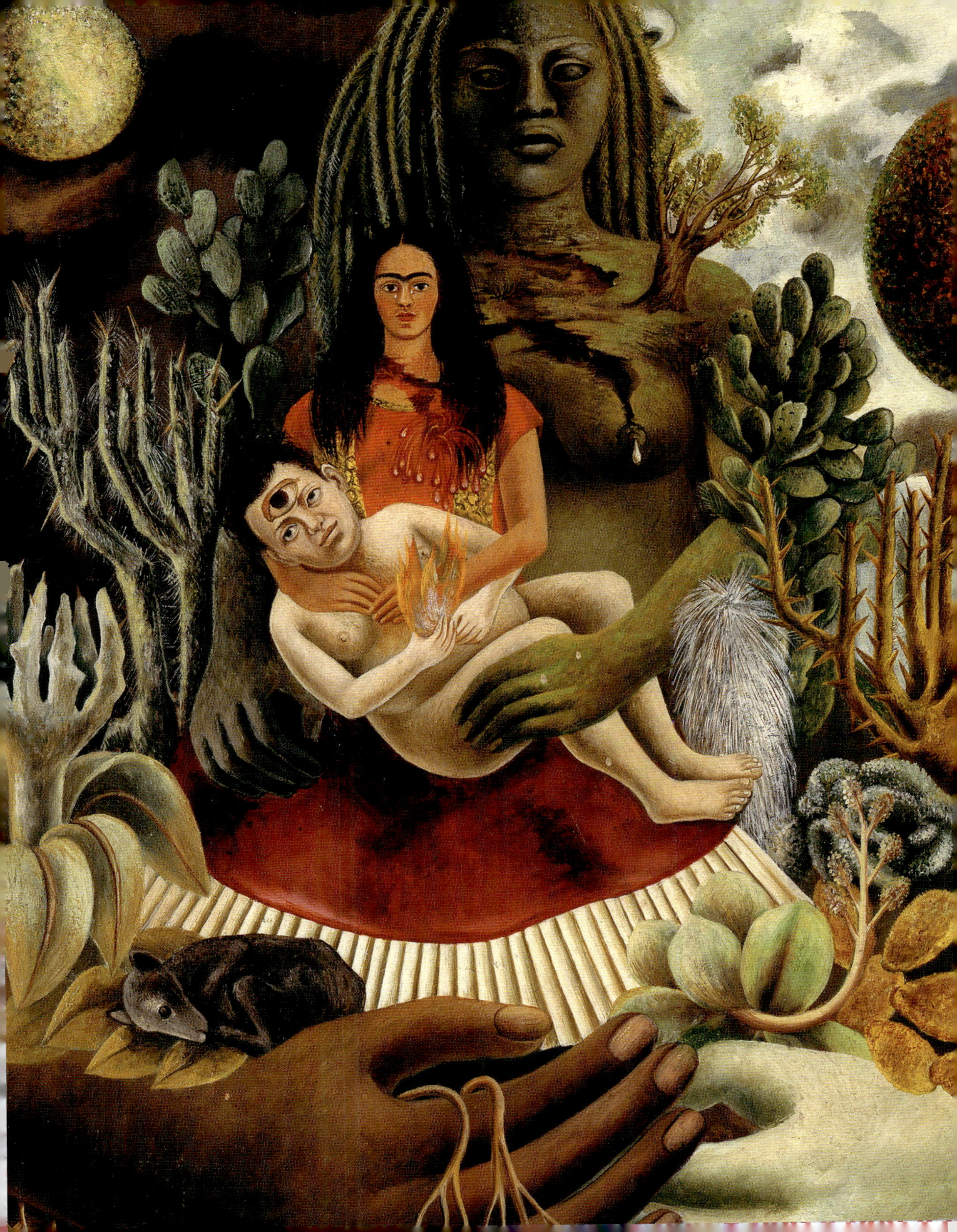